I0797289

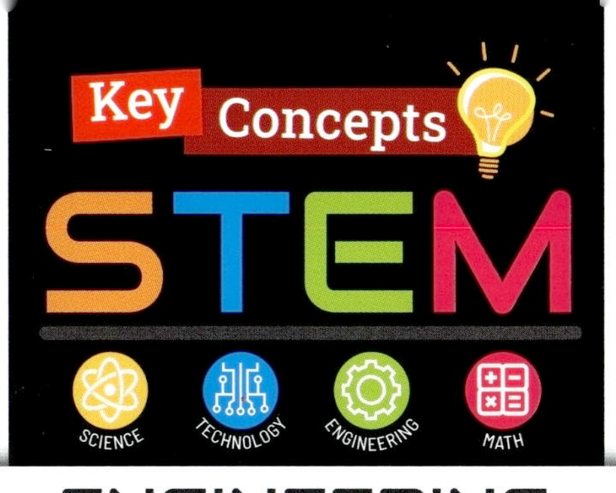

ENGINEERING AND TECHNOLOGY

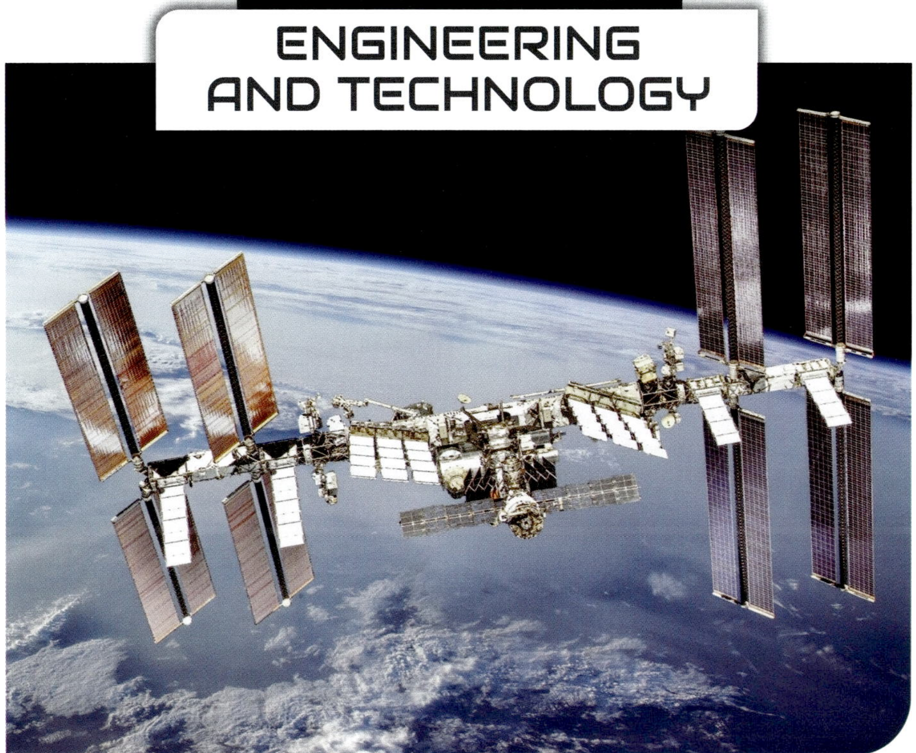

AIR AND SPACE

General Editor: Anne O'Daly

Published by Brown Bear Books Ltd
4877 N. Circulo Bujia, Tucson, AZ 85718
USA
and
Studio G14, Regent Studios, 1 Thane Villas,
London N7 7PH, UK

Cataloging-in-Publication data available upon request.

ISBN 978-1-83572-060-8 (ALB)
ISBN 978-1-83572-066-0 (paperback)
ISBN 978-1-83572-072-1 (ebook)

Children's Publisher: Anne O'Daly
Design Manager: Keith Davis
Picture Manager: Sophie Mortimer
Consultant: Chris Woodford

Manufactured in the United States of America
CPSIA compliance information: Batch#AG/5664

Picture Credits
Front Cover: Shutterstock: ArtsiomP. **Interior: Dreamstime:** MakanaCreative 15; **iStock:** dottedhippo 52, Ultima_Galina 4; **Library of Congress:** 6, 7, 60; **NASA IMAGES:** 54, 55t, Armes Research Center/NASA-ARC 56, DFRC 28, Earth 40t, ESA 59b, Goddard SC/John Hopkins University 59t, GRIN 26t, 42l, 42r, 51b, Kennedy Space Center 57, Photojournal.jpl 50, 53, 58, 61, Cornell University/Maas Digital LLC 55b; **Photos.com:** 14, 16; **Public Domain:** 5, 24l, AAxanderr 37, National Archief/Spaarnestad Photo/Sam Shere 10, Towpilot 21; **Shutterstock:** 13l, Andrey 49, Aphelleon 46l, Gordon Bell 25r, BlueBarronPhoto 32b, Paul Brewer 29, Ryan Fletcher 30, 31, Martin Charles Hatch 18t, melissamn 18b, Alejo Miranda 51t, NASA 44r, Nerthuz 44l, Patrick Photo 36, A Periam Photography 35, Dario Sabljak 46b, John Selway 32t, TanyaJoy 12, Michael W NZ 20, De Visu 25b, Jason Wells 34b, Sam Whitfield1 22, Dima Zel /NASA 1, 48; **Thinkstock:** Hemrea 40b, 43; **Topfoto:** Flight Collection 29inset, Roger-Viollet 24r, ullsteinbild 8, 61t; **United States Government:** Department of Defense 34t, USAF photo 23, 26b.

STEM

Key Concepts in STEM: Engineering and Technology describes the scientific principles and feats of engineering that have shaped the world we live in. Since earliest times, people have created tools and machines to provide shelter, warmth, prosperity, security, and protection from disease. This book looks at the history of flight. In the 18th century the Montgolfier brothers flew a hot-air balloon for the first time. Aircraft powered by engines followed. Over the past century, jet-powered aircraft and powerful rockets have enabled people to go to the Moon—with the real possibility of going far beyond in the not too distant future. Explanatory diagrams and informative photographs explain how STEM (science, technology, engineering, and math) has transformed our lives and continues to influence our world today.

Contents

FLYING WITHOUT WINGS

From ancient times, people looked at the skies, watching birds fly and dreaming of a time when humans might be able to fly as well. The technology that allowed this to happen took centuries to perfect.

There had been many attempts to fly before balloons were invented, but these had usually involved trying to imitate the flight of birds using artificial wings. All these attempts had ended in failure, sometimes fatally for the flyer. In China, kites had been invented about 500 BCE, and it is known that sometimes people were strapped to kites and went airborne. In China also, the principle of using hot air to send paper balloons into the sky was known as early as 300 BCE.

The major development that contributed to the first controlled flights came in the early modern period in Europe. This was due to a better understanding of the nature of gases, including the air. Through the work of pioneers such as Anglo-Irish chemist Robert

Many people take a flight in a hot-air balloon to see spectacular views. However, hot-air balloons are difficult to steer and move wherever the wind takes them.

Boyle (1627–1691), people came to realize that different gases had different weights, and that the gas contained in a "bubble" would rise if it was lighter than the gas outside the bubble.

The Montgolfier Brothers

On a sunny June day in 1783, French brothers Joseph-Michel (1740–1810) and Jacques-Étienne (1745–1799) Montgolfier unveiled a new invention in the marketplace in Annonay, southern France. The brothers burned straw and wood under a specially designed bag. Thrilled onlookers watched open mouthed as

BALLOONS IN EAST ASIA

More than 2,000 years ago, Chinese children played a game that created tiny hot-air balloons. The children placed a few dry twigs inside empty eggshells and set the twigs alight to send the eggshells flying.

Centuries later, in the 1200s, the Mongol people from the wide open plains of Central Asia would launch a dragon-shaped hot-air balloon to mark rallying points. The first ascent of a hot-air balloon in the Western world, however, did not take place until about 500 years later.

NAZCA BALLOONISTS

Between 500 BCE and 900 CE, the people of the Nazca culture drew huge figures on the desert plains, near the coast of Peru in South America. Many of these gigantic pictures of animals can only be seen from the air. Some scientists believe that the Nazca people knew how to fly in balloons to view the images. Nazca potters often decorated their pots with pictures of balloons and kites, and Nazca textiles show pictures of flying men.

In the 1970s, Nazca fabrics were tested by a modern balloon-making company. The company found that the traditional fabrics had a tighter weave than the material the company used themselves, making them ideal for hot-air ballooning. In 1975, the International Explorers Society of Miami made their own balloon, *Condor I*, based on Peruvian designs and materials. The balloon was filled with hot smoke produced by burning dry wood. Scorched circles of rock found near the giant artworks might have been created by similar fires centuries ago. *Condor I* rose 380 ft (116 m) into the air and descended safely after several minutes. This doesn't prove that the ancient Peruvians knew how to fly, but it does prove that it was possible.

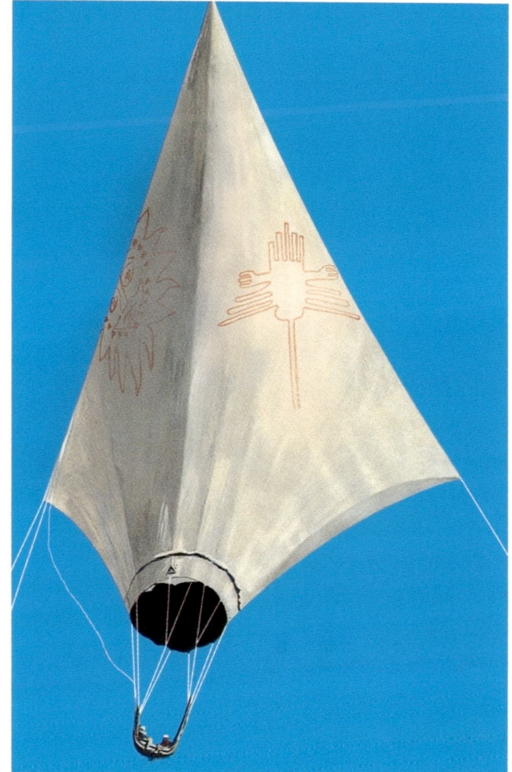

A two-person crew tested Condor I, *sitting in a cradle made from bundles of reeds.*

HUMAN FLIGHT

On September 19, 1783, the Montgolfiers repeated their demonstration at the royal palace of Versailles, France. This time, they sent a sheep, a duck, and a chicken into the air. The balloon floated for about eight minutes and then returned safely to Earth.

The demonstration was watched by the Marquis d'Arlandes (1742–1809) and his friend Jean-François Pilâtre de Rozier (1757–1785). The two men then set about becoming the first people to take to the skies in a free-floating hot-air balloon. On a crisp, clear November day in 1783, the two men climbed into the skies over Paris in a Montgolfier balloon. They burned straw and wool to keep the balloon in the air. Their 5.5 mile (9 km) journey above the city lasted around 25 minutes. Two years later, Pilâtre de Rozier was killed when his balloon exploded as he was attempting to cross the English Channel.

The flight of the Montgolfier brothers' first balloon in Annonay, France, was watched by a large audience.

the Western world's first hot-air balloon soared 3,000 ft (910 m) into the air, although it was tethered to the ground. A few months later they repeated the display in front of the French king and queen, only this time they sent three farm animals up in a basket under the balloon. A few months later, balloons were carrying people high into the air.

The First Airship

It was not possible to steer the earliest hot-air balloons. There was no power source small enough and light enough to fit in a balloon's basket. Balloons were at the mercy of the winds, unless tethered to the ground.

As engines of various kinds were invented during the Industrial Revolution of the 19th century, attempts were made to fit engines into balloons. In particular, every military power that could afford such a program was rushing to build a "warship of the air." It was Frenchman Henri Giffard (1825–1882) who was the first person to create such an aircraft. As early as 1852, Giffard designed and built the world's first "dirigible" (from the French word *diriger*, meaning "to steer"). Rather than use a normal circular-shaped bag, Giffard used an elongated cigar-shaped bag full of hydrogen. His ship was powered by a steam engine weighing 350 lb (150 kg), so Giffard had to use a gas bag 144 ft (44 m) long. He started out from Paris on his first flight and traveled 17 miles (27 km), reaching a top speed of 6 mph (10 km/h).

Unfortunately for Giffard, however, his craft was fated always to be underpowered. Although his dirigible was a significant improvement on the ordinary balloon, any aircraft possessing a top speed of 6 mph (10 km/h) was always going to be uncontrollable in wind speeds of 7 mph (11 km/h) or more.

PUTTING BALLOONS TO WORK

While balloons provided entertaining diversions from the routine of 18th-century life, they appeared at first to have no practical use. One man, however, soon realized that he could use tethered balloons to his advantage. French general Napoleon Bonaparte (1769–1821), who later became the emperor of France, formed the world's first ever military airborne division. Known as the Aérostiers, this intrepid group of balloonists used balloons that were tethered to the ground so they could not float away. They gave the French Army an advantage by revealing the exact location of enemy troops. Tethered balloons were used by many armies, including both sides during the American Civil War (1861–1865).

A hydrogen balloon, known as Intrepid, *is inflated by a surveillance unit during the American Civil War. A spotter aboard the balloon gave reports on the movements of enemy forces while a rope attached to the ground kept the balloon from floating away.*

This situation improved in 1872, when German engineer Paul Haenlein (1835–1905) fitted the recently invented (and much lighter) internal-combustion engine to a dirigible.

To save weight, Haenlein used the super-light hydrogen gas in the balloon as fuel, although it reduced the distance it could travel before it began to lose height. In 1883, brothers Albert (1839–1906) and Gaston (1843–1899) Tissandier powered a dirigible with an electric motor.

Zeppelins

The greatest dirigible designer was Count Ferdinand von Zeppelin (1838–1917). Zeppelin had been a cavalryman in the Prussian (German) army and a volunteer for the Union Army in the American Civil War. While he was in the United States, Zeppelin flew in hot-air balloons and devoted the rest of his life to building bigger and better flying machines. Zeppelin added a lightweight frame to the gas bag, making it more rigid, so that the dirigible would remain controllable at higher speeds. On July 2, 1900, Zeppelin took his early "airship" on its first flight, over Lake Constance in Germany. The flight lasted for

SCIENCE WORDS

Atom: The smallest units in a substance.
Dense: A description of how much mass is packed into a substance.
Hydrogen: A highly flammable gas that is lighter than air.
Internal-combustion: The engine system used in cars and trucks.

USING HYDROGEN

The French physicist Jacques-Alexandre Charles (1746–1823) fellow Frenchman Nicolas-Louis Robert (1760–1820) used a different gas to take to the air. Just six months after the Montgolfier brothers first demonstrated their hot-air balloon, Charles and Robert set out in a balloon that had been filled with hydrogen (the lightest of all gases). Once the balloon was released, the two men shot nearly one mile (1.6 km) up into the sky. Charles and Robert eventually returned safely to the ground by using a release valve to let out hydrogen. Despite their early scare they made many more flights.

just 17 minutes before *Luftschiff Zeppelin One* (LZ-1), as he called the machine, dropped to the surface of the lake. It was another eight years before Zeppelin's first truly successful flight, with LZ-4. At the time LZ-4 was the largest airship in the skies. It was an incredible 446 ft (136 m) long and required 500,000 cubic ft (14,000 m3) of hydrogen to get off the ground. On July 4, 1908, LZ-4 traveled at 40 mph (60 km/h) for 12 hours over Switzerland. At last, a practical, powered, controllable form of air travel had arrived.

The Graf Zeppelin *(LZ-127) made 590 flights between 1928 and 1937 and traveled more than a million miles in its lifetime. It was broken up in 1940.*

HOW BALLOONS AND AIRSHIPS FLY

To fly, airships and balloons need to generate enough lift to counteract gravity, which is constantly pulling them back to Earth. The Montgolfier brothers knew that hot air rises and they realized that they could make a balloon go up by filling it with hot gas. When they heated ordinary air, the minute gas particles (made of atoms) began to move around faster and spread out. This made the air inside the balloon less dense than the cold air around it, making the balloon lighter than the surrounding air, and so it floated upward. When the air cooled, the balloon returned to the ground again. Jacques-Alexandre Charles was also aware of the principles of lighter-than-air flight. He reasoned, however, that it should be possible to take to the skies by filling a balloon with a gas that was naturally less dense than air at normal temperatures. Gases such as helium or hydrogen, for example, are made up from particles that are much smaller and lighter than those of the oxygen and nitrogen gases that make up the air.

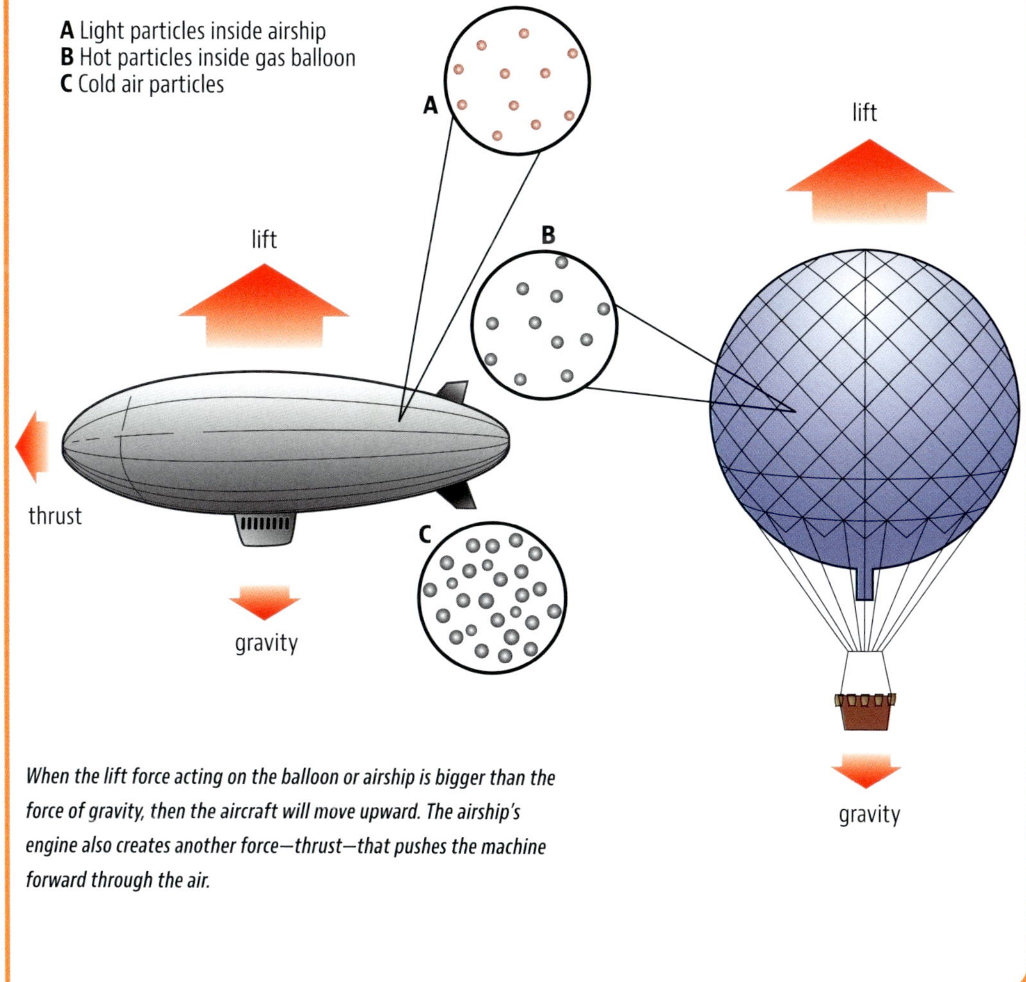

When the lift force acting on the balloon or airship is bigger than the force of gravity, then the aircraft will move upward. The airship's engine also creates another force—thrust—that pushes the machine forward through the air.

The Hindenburg *exploded while docking at the Lakehurst Air Station in New Jersey in 1937. The explosion was probably caused by a spark of static electricity that ignited the hydrogen bags.*

AIRSHIPS AS AIRLINERS

In the 1920s there were few planes that could offer the same long-distance travel opportunities as airships. Large airships, such as the British *R101*, were equipped to carry passengers over long distances, carried in gondolas positioned below the main gas bags. Airships had to be light, so they were made from light materials, such as aluminum. Travelers could view the world below from promenades, which were closed in with windows made from lightweight plastic alternatives to glass. Unfortunately, in October 1930 the *R101* crashed on its first flight, killing all but 6 of the 54 people on board. Similar fatal crashes made it clear that hydrogen airships were just too dangerous.

Between 1910 and the outbreak of World War I in 1914, about 34,000 people had their first taste of air travel in a Zeppelin airship. The war spurred on airship construction, and Germany led the world in airship design, building 88 military airships. London, England, was the first city to be attacked from the air when a group of "zeppelins" made a raid during World War I.

The End of the Airship

Between 1920 and 1933, the U.S. Navy built five airships. Three of them crashed: the *Shenandoah* (1925), the *Akron* (1933), and the *Macon* (1935). In 1936, Germany's *Hindenburg* began making regular transatlantic crossings. Unfortunately for all concerned, this proved to be the final chapter in the history of the airship. Although hydrogen is the lightest of all gases, it is also one of the most flammable. The *Hindenburg* crashed tragically the

NONRIGID AND RIGID AIRSHIPS

Nonrigid airships (or blimps) have no internal framework to support the shape of the outer envelope, which is filled with gas and one or more air-filled ballonets. Air can be released from the ballonets or pumped in to increase or decrease lift. Rigid airships (or zeppelins) have an internal framework that supports the outer envelope. The zeppelin was almost (but not quite) a successful technology.

NONRIGID AIRSHIP

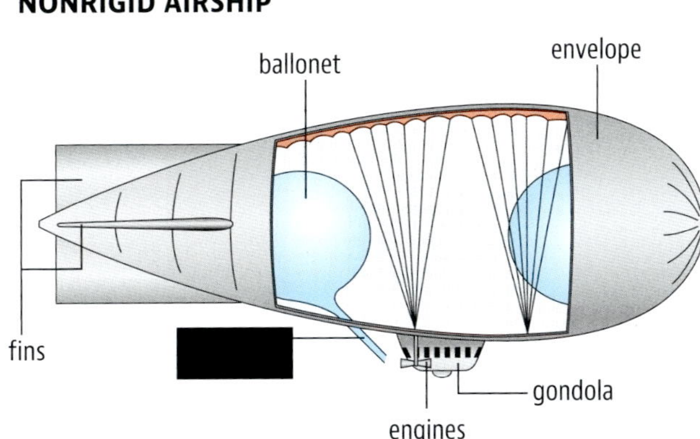

RIGID AIRSHIP

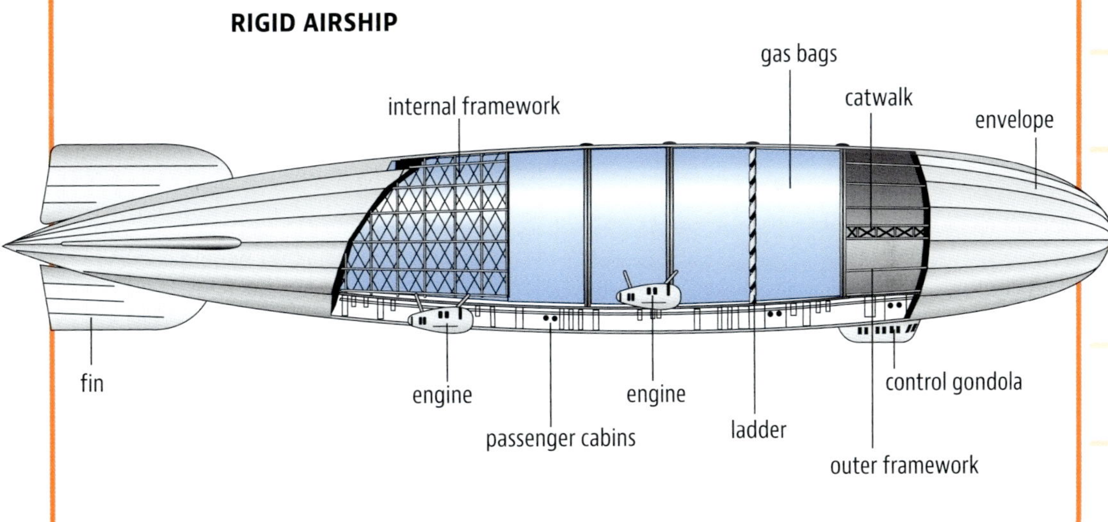

following year, and airships of this size were never built again.

Today, scientists use hydrogen gas balloons to take equipment high into the sky to study the upper atmosphere and weather conditions. Modern airships are filled with helium gas, which is slightly heavier than hydrogen but much safer. Helium blimps are often used to tow flying advertisements at sports games and other large public events.

FACTS AND FIGURES

- *Hindenburg* was the largest rigid airship ever built, at 804 ft (245 m) long. It held over 7,000,000 cubic feet (roughly 200,000 m^3) of hydrogen gas.
- In 1929, the *Graf Zeppelin* made the first round-the-world airship flight in just 21 days, 5 hours, and 54 minutes.

THE AGE OF PROPELLERS

It took another 120 years of invention after the first balloonists had floated into the air for winged aircraft to finally take to the skies. This was the beginning of powered flight.

The first fixed-wing aircraft were powered by propeller engines. A spinning propeller's shape pushes air backward—and the airplane forward—in much the same way as a ship's propeller moves a vessel through water.

Hot-air balloons and gas-filled airships only fly because they are lighter than air. Balloons are at the mercy of the wind, and while airships could be steered, they were slow and very dangerous. People could still only dream of flying in safe, fast, controllable craft. However, long before the last of the great hydrogen-filled airships had come to a terrible and fiery end, the skies were buzzing with a new sound.

The First Pioneers

Before the invention of hot-air and gas balloons, it had been assumed that if humans were to fly, it would be by imitating birds. Optimistic inventors designed aircraft fitted with flapping wings. But in 1680, Italian scientist Giovanni A. Borelli (1608–1679) finally proved that the human chest muscles were not big enough to flap wings the size that would be needed to lift people off the ground and into the air.

LEONARDO DA VINCI

Italian artist and scientist Leonardo da Vinci (1452–1519) dreamed of taking to the air in all manner of devices. His drawings included plans for an airplane, a simple parachute, and this sail-powered helicopter.

Da Vinci imagined his helicopter's screw-shaped sail would pull the craft into the air when it was spun around.

It was not until 1804 that the first working model of an aircraft with fixed wings was made, by British scientist George Cayley (1773–1857). Cayley's glider also had a rigid body (or fuselage) and a tail with a rudder and moveable control surfaces that could be used to send the craft up or down. He had established the basic structure of modern airplanes. Cayley spent the next 50 years testing his ideas before building a full-sized glider. Finally, in 1853, Cayley's coachman took to the air in the first ever successful flight of a full-sized glider and the first successful use of the curved "airfoil" wing shape. All Cayley's glider needed to become a plane was an engine and propeller. Unfortunately, those engines that existed at the time were too heavy, large, and inefficient.

Many other engineers also contributed to the development of gliders, such as the American Octave Chanute (1832–1910), who wrote *Progress of Flying Machines* (1895), and the German Otto Lilienthal (1848–1896), who recorded his research in *Bird Flight as the Basis of Aviation* (1889).

OTTO LILIENTHAL

Otto Lilienthal was a German aeronautical pioneer and the first person to make controlled glider flights. He was born in Prussia, now Germany, in 1848. Lilienthal developed an interest in flying when still a boy, studying bird flight and making models. He served in the army during the Franco-Prussian War (1870–71) and then worked in industry as an engineer.

Lilienthal researched bird flight and wing shapes in the 1860s and 1870s. By 1891 he had built a full-sized glider that he strapped to his arms. He took off by running downhill until he was airborne and controlled the glider by swinging his body from side to side. He made around 2,000 successful flights, some up to 330 yards (300 m) long, in more than 16 different gliders. The gliders included biplanes (with two wings), and he planned one with a carbon dioxide gas motor to flap the wings.

Lilienthal crashed in a glider on August 9, 1896, and died the next day in hospital. News of his flights were published around the world, and he inspired many other inventors.

The Wright Brothers

The work of Chanute and Lilienthal inspired two brothers in Dayton, Ohio. Having studied the work of Cayley and Lilienthal, bicycle makers and printers Wilbur (1867–1912) and Orville (1871–1948) Wright set about designing controllable gliders. From watching buzzards in flight, the brothers knew that a successful aircraft would have to be able to bank to one side or another, climb or descend, and turn from left to right.

The last glider built by the Wright brothers in 1902, could perform all these movements. They had also built a wind tunnel to test the aerodynamics of the glider's wing and surface shape. Now all that remained was to add a lightweight engine and propeller so the machine could power its own takeoff, flight, and landing.

Previous engineers had tried to power planes with heavy steam engines, but the Wright brothers were able to make use of the recently invented internal-combustion engine. They designed and built a small gasoline engine and connected it to a pair of propellers

German aviator Otto Lilienthal built gliders with curved wings to create lift. Some of the gliders were large enough to carry him, but Lilienthal died in a crash in 1896.

AIRFOIL SHAPE AND LIFT FORCE

The design of the airfoil wing allows an airplane to move upward using the forward thrust of the engine. For many decades, scientists believed that this was due to a scientific theory known as Bernoulli's principle. Swiss mathematician and physicist Daniel Bernoulli (1700–1782) had shown that the pressure of a fluid (gas or liquid) decreases as its speed increases. Bernoulli's theory indicated to other scientists that if the speed of air passing over the wing was greater than that of the air passing under the wing, a pressure difference, if great enough, would cause the wing to lift upward. However, it is now known that the lift is explained by Isaac Newton's Third Law of Motion—for every action, there is an equal and opposite reaction. The airfoil works to give lift because the air stays close to the curve at the top of the wing and is then thrown out down and behind the wing.

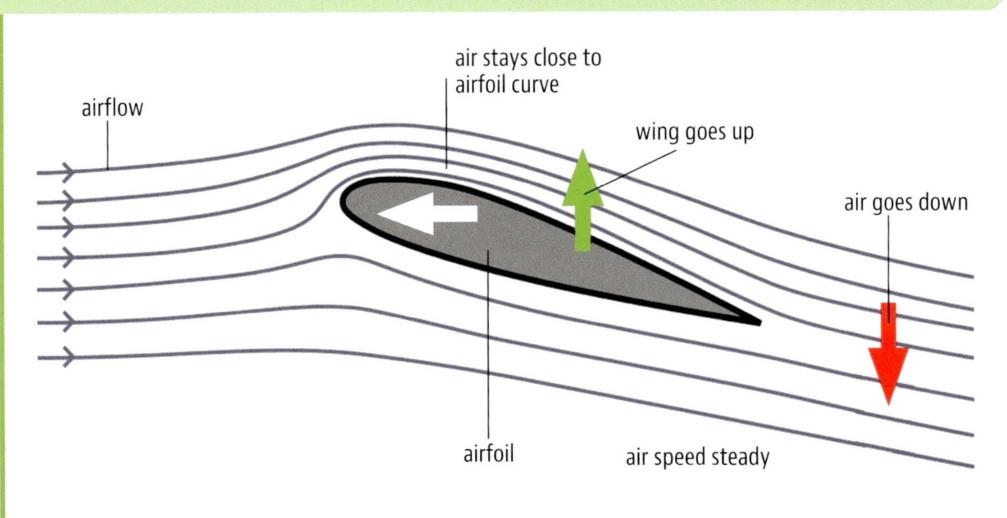

KITES: THE FIRST WINGED AIRCRAFT

The first heavier-than-air craft to be flown were probably kites. The ancient Chinese discovered how to make kites between 400 and 300 BCE. A few hundred years later the Chinese authorities strapped criminals to enormous kites, sending them high into the skies. More than 2,000 years later Lawrence Hargrave (1850–1915), an Australian draftsman, began to experiment with kites. In 1894, he was lifted 16 ft (5 m) off the ground by four box kites of his own making.

Some people have claimed that Hargrave's work had little impact on the history of flight since he was working in Australia, cut off from the mainstream of aviation history in the United States and Europe. However, many of Hargrave's ideas were used in early aircraft: the wings of many early planes resembled box kites, for example. Like other early aviators, Hargrave also confirmed that wings with curved surfaces (airfoils) flew better than flat wings.

Kites fly using the same principles as fixed-winged aircraft.

(which they had also designed) using bicycle chains. Their glider was now an airplane.

On December 17, 1903, Orville Wright took off from level ground in the first powered airplane—*Flyer I* (popularly known as Kitty Hawk). The Wright brothers continued to experiment with airplanes throughout 1904, making a number of improvements in the way the original aircraft handled. In 1905 the brothers built *Flyer III*—the world's first practical airplane. It could turn, bank, circle, fly figures of eight, and remain airborne for more than half an hour.

The Wright brothers refused to fly again until they got financial backing from the government or a private company. In 1908 the United States government issued a contract to the Wright brothers for an airplane that could carry a pilot and an observer for 125 miles (200 km). The brothers delivered such an aircraft one year later. Their plane was a remarkable improvement on the technology that just six years earlier had only been capable of carrying a single aviator for 170 ft (51.5 m). Within a year every major army in the world had a force of airplanes.

Unlike modern airplanes, the Wright brothers' Flyer 1 *had elevators at the front instead of on the tail. In addition, the steering system used wires to bend the wings to alter the way lift acted on the aircraft.*

War and Technology

It is one of the unfortunate truths of history that technology always takes massive leaps forward during wartime because new weapons can tip the balance from defeat to victory. Although originally conceived as a means of spying on the enemy, military airplanes were soon fitted with weapons. October 30, 1911, marks the day when modern air war began. An Italian pilot on a spying mission over Libya during a war between Italy and Turkey took it upon himself to drop four hand grenades onto the enemy trenches below, thereby changing forever the way war

FACTS AND FIGURES

- Orville Wright's first powered flight in *Flyer I* lasted just 12 seconds. He traveled 170 ft (51.5 m), which included the takeoff and the landing run.
- *Flyer I* had a 12-horsepower (9 kilowatt) engine, a maximum speed of roughly 30 mph (50 km/h), and a wingspan of 40 ft (12 m).

would, in future, be waged. By the time World War I (1914–1918) broke out in Europe, all sides were equipped with warplanes.

Biplanes

The stresses placed on an airplane during combat are far greater than those experienced during normal passenger flights. The greatest problem facing aircraft manufacturers at that time was how to design airplanes that were both lightweight and strong. Several designs, using between one and four sets of wings, were tested, but the design that best met the requirements of lightness and strength was the biplane.

The biplane design stacks one wing on top of another to create a boxlike structure. The real beauty of the biplane design was the way struts and bracing wires were cleverly arranged to take advantage of the inbuilt strength of triangular-based structures. By running bracing wires diagonally from the base of a strut on the lower wing to the top of a strut on the upper wing, it was possible to create a structure so rigid that it would collapse only on impact with something solid (often the ground). The only drawback of the biplane was that twin wings, bracing wires, and struts caused a great deal of drag, slowing the plane down and increasing fuel consumption. Nevertheless, biplanes pushed back the boundaries of aviation. In 1919, two British pilots flew across the Atlantic Ocean in a large Vickers biplane, taking under 17 hours to fly from the island of Newfoundland to Ireland.

Monoplanes

As new ultrastrong yet lightweight materials were being created, it became possible to design airplanes with single wings—called monoplanes. The first practical monoplane had been built as early as 1907 by French engineer Louis Blériot (1872–1936), who flew an improved version of this plane across the English Channel two years later. In 1927, U.S. Airmail pilot Charles Lindbergh (1902–1974), now one of the best-known figures in aviation history, made the first nonstop solo flight across the Atlantic in the monoplane *Spirit of St. Louis*. Monoplane design was not widely adopted, however, until World War II (1939–1945).

FORCES ACTING ON A PLANE

To be able to fly, an airplane has to generate enough lift and thrust to overcome gravity, which is constantly pulling the plane back toward Earth, and drag (the resistance of the air to objects passing through it). The airfoil (curved) shape of an airplane's wing enables it to generate lift; thrust is generated by the airplane's engine and, if it has them, propellers, which act like airfoils. For a glider to fly, it has to be towed until it reaches a speed at which its wings are generating enough lift to fly. The pilots of the first gliders had to run down slopes and use the wind to take off. On aircraft carriers, catapults create powerful initial thrust.

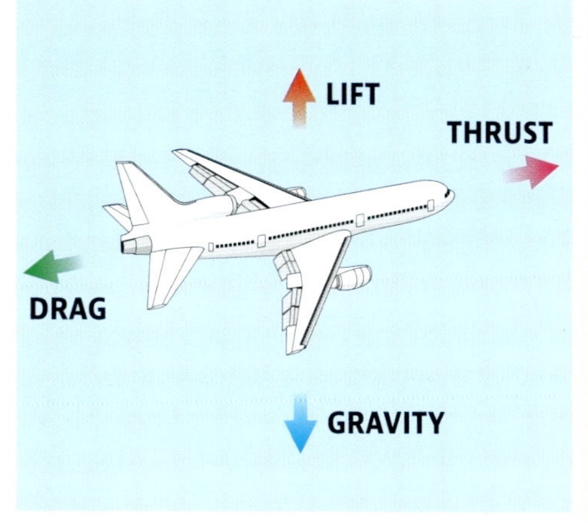

A biplane's super-strong construction makes it ideal for performing spectacular acrobatic maneuvers that would destroy faster but less robust aircraft.

SEAPLANES AND FLYING BOATS

Seaplanes are aircraft that can land on and take off from water. Instead of wheels—or as well as wheels—the undercarriage has large floats. The first seaplane was built by Henri Fabre (1882–1984) in France in 1910. A flying boat is a type of seaplane that is supported on the water by its main body, which is hull-shaped, like a boat. The first flying boat was flown by American aviation pioneer Glenn Curtiss (1878–1930) in 1912. In the 1930s, flying boats were used for international travel: there was a shortage of airports outside North America and Europe, so flying boats were ideal since they did not need airports. By the 1950s, however, flying boats had largely been replaced by land-based aircraft. Until the arrival of helicopters, flying boats were also used in air–sea rescues.

Aircraft with floats attached to the undercarriage are ideal transportation in rugged mountain regions, where there are few runways—or even roads—but plenty of large lakes to land on.

LIGHT AIRPLANES

Modern light planes vary little from the design of early monoplanes. Most have a single engine that drives a propeller, and can seat from one to ten people. However, instead of being built from wood and fabric, today's light aircraft are made from metals or strong plastics. They rarely weigh more than 12,000 pounds (5,500 kg).

The basic parts of a light airplane are the wings, fuselage (body), tail assembly, and landing gear. Light planes, such as Cessnas and Pipers, are a widely used form of transportation in the United States and sparsely populated countries where there are huge distances between cities, such as Canada and Australia.

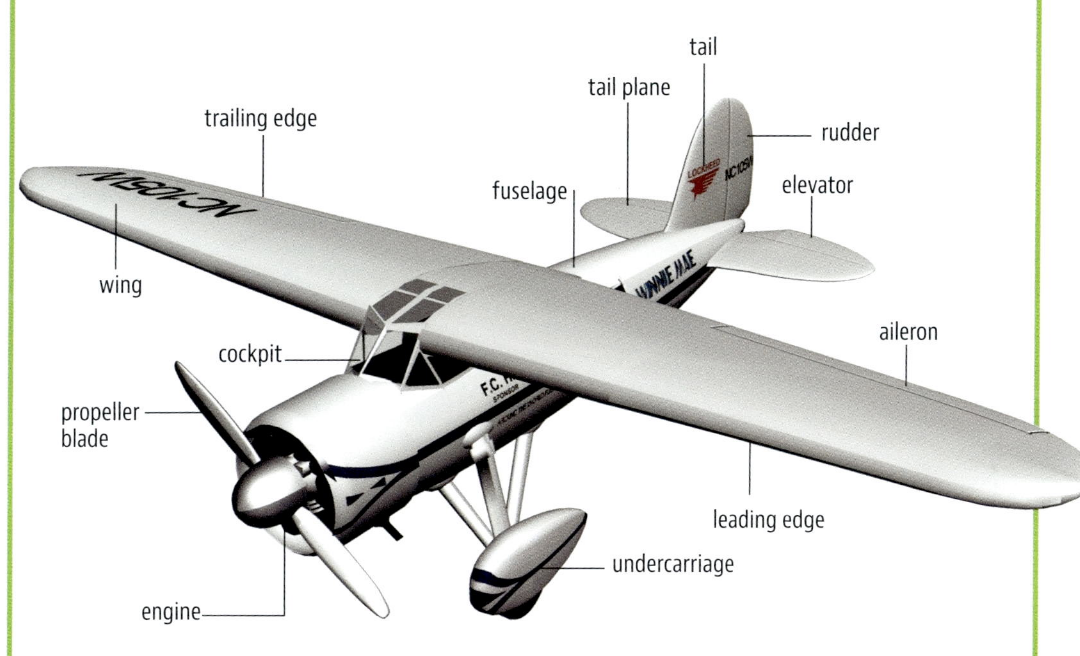

The wings and tail planes have an airfoil shape. The pilot steers using moveable flaps on the back—or trailing—edges of the wings, which direct the air flowing over the plane.

Since World War II, virtually every plane built has been a monoplane. Another major advance was made in materials. The earliest planes were made from wood and fabric and the 1920s saw fabric-covered metal-framed planes. All-metal planes were introduced during the war, when it also soon became clear that no side could win a battle unless it had control of the air. Small, agile so-called "fighter" aircraft fought fierce air battles to

SCIENCE WORDS

Airfoil: The curved shape of a wing that is needed to create a lift force.

Aviator: A person who flies aircraft.

Fuselage: The body of an airplane, containing the cockpit and passenger cabin.

Wingspan: The distance from one wing tip to the other.

The Messerschmitt Bf 109, often known as the Me-109, was the main fighter plane used by the German air force (Luftwaffe) during World War II.

decide who would take control. The first important battle to be fought entirely in the air was the Battle of Britain in 1940. During the battle, the German air force tried to assert air superiority over southern Britain to cover an invasion attempt over the English Channel.

The battle for air control was as much a battle between opposing airplane designs as it was between opposite sides in the war: Supermarine Aviation's Spitfire and the Hawker (later British Aerospace) company's Hurricane were pitted against the less romantically named Bf 109, made by German company Messerschmitt. When the United States and Japan entered the war at the end of 1941, the Japanese company Mitsubishi supplied the remarkable A6M. Known to the Allies as the Zero, this fighter made the best of a small engine by being the strongest and lightest fighter in the war. Initially it outclassed any United States' fighter it came up against.

By the end of World War II in 1945, the propeller-driven airplane had reached the limit of its design capabilities. If airplanes were to get any faster, they would need a new kind of engine. The jet age was about to dawn.

FACTS AND FIGURES

- The 1927 Lockheed Vega, a monoplane, had a wingspan of 41 ft (12.5 m) and a 425-horsepower (318 kilowatt) engine.
- The Hughes H-4 Hercules flying boat, or "Spruce Goose," had a wingspan of 321 ft (97.5 m), the largest of any aircraft. Built in 1947, this giant wooden plane flew only once, covering approximately 1 mile (1.6 km).

SOCIETY AND INVENTIONS

The First Modern Airliners

In 1933, the American company Boeing designed the Boeing 247. Previous airliners (passenger- or freight-carrying planes) were limited in how far they could fly and how many people they could carry. The Boeing 247 marked a revolution in airliner design. Fast, with a cruising speed of 180 mph (300 km/h), it could travel for up to 750 miles (1,200 km) before it had to stop for more fuel. Two years later, the Douglas Aircraft Company launched the DC-3, which could outfly the 247 and cover 1,000 miles (1,600 km) in less than five hours. The DC-3, or Dakota as it is also known, was the major commercial airliner worldwide until the 1950s.

More than 16,000 DC-3s were built for use as airliners and cargo planes. More than 150 are still used today. The plane was much wider than earlier passenger aircraft. It could carry up to 32 passengers, sitting in rows of four seats.

THE JET AGE AND BEYOND

The invention of the jet engine brought about a revolution in flight. Jet-propelled aircraft were powerful enough to move faster than sound itself, fly to the edge of space, and hover in midair.

As the 1920s came to an end, a few of the pioneering airplane designers had begun to realize that there was nowhere left for them to go. A greater understanding of how objects move through the air—the science of aerodynamics—had inevitably led to sleeker, faster aircraft that could cut through the sky without being damaged. However, it was becoming apparent that the normal arrangement of engine and propeller was an inadequate power source for the future requirements of modern aviation.

PROPELLER LIMITATIONS

As faster, more powerful aircraft were developed, airplane designers had to consider the medium through which their aircraft flew. With early designs, the air passing over the surfaces of an airplane had behaved like a fluid, flowing around the craft and providing the necessary lift to keep the plane off the ground. Now, with more powerful machines, engineers realized that at speeds approaching 700 mph (1,100 km/h) air behaves differently. Drag (air resistance) on the airplane increases to the point at which the air makes shock waves that buffet the aircraft body. This reduces lift so much that the pilot loses control. An airplane's propellers always move faster than the rest of the craft, so propellers are the first part of the airplane to suffer from this problem. In effect, the behavior of the air around the propeller imposes a strict limit on the speeds that can be reached by aircraft powered by them.

THE NEED FOR SPEED

The fastest planes in regular use are military jets, such as this Eurofighter Typhoon. It has a top speed of 1,550 mph (2,495 km/h). This speed is achieved using afterburners, which burn more fuel in the hot exhaust to create an extra boost and more thrust for the aircraft.

ROCKET PLANES

Before the jet engine was widely adopted, scientists experimented with using rocket engines to make planes travel faster. In Germany as early as 1928, Alexander M. Lippisch (1894–1976) had designed the world's first successful rocket plane. It was a tailless glider fitted with two rocket engines that used solid fuel. The first operational liquid-fuel rocket plane, the Messerschmitt Me-163 Komet (below), drew heavily on Lippisch's design. The Komet could reach speeds of more than 600 mph (970 km/h), but it could not fly for long and often exploded on landing. Military aircraft manufacturers have since occasionally built rocket planes, mostly to carry out research at high speeds and to high altitudes. The Bell X-1, for example, was the first plane to fly faster than the speed of sound. The American X-15 rocket plane flew over 310,000 ft (over 95,000 m, or 95 km) above Earth in 1962 and later traveled at five times the speed of sound.

New Engines

The military's need for faster aircraft encouraged the development of new engines. In the 1930s, scientists in both the United States and Germany were investigating the possibility of using rockets as airplane engines. The German researchers were led by Wernher von Braun (1912–1977) and the Americans by Robert Hutchings Goddard (1882–1945). However, rocket engines were expensive to fuel, were hard to control, and frequently exploded.

In Britain engineer Frank Whittle (1907–1996) patented the jet engine in 1930. He joined up with a handful of friends and formed a company called Power Jets Ltd. By 1937, Whittle and his associates had built an operational jet engine in their workshop. The jet age was dawning. But it was not until the 1950s that the jet engine came into widespread use when people realized that as well as making planes go faster, jet engines could reduce the cost of air travel. Whittle's invention used a jet of hot gases to push the aircraft along. The stream of gases was produced by drawing air into the engine using a fanlike turbine. The air was then used to burn some fuel inside a central combustion chamber, producing the blast of hot exhaust gases that created the thrust.

The First Jet Airplane

The British government was reluctant to fund Whittle's research. They threw away the opportunity to be the first military power to build a jet-powered airplane, and the honor went, instead, to the German-based company Heinkel. Working independently of Frank Whittle, three German engineers—Hans von Ohain, Herbert Wagner, and Helmut Schelp—had investigated the idea of the jet engine. On August 27, 1939, the Heinkel He-178, powered by a jet engine designed by von Ohain, took to the skies over Germany.

The British government did not take Whittle's idea seriously until the outbreak of World War II (1939–1945), giving the Germans a two-year head start in jet-engine technology. In 1944, the British government took over Power Jets Ltd, just in time to see the Gloster Meteor, the Royal Air Force's first operational jet fighter, go into battle against the German Messerschmitt's jet-powered Me-262. By the time World War II ended in 1945, it was clear to all sides that military combat planes were going to have to be jet

COANDA'S AIRCRAFT

In 1910, a Romanian inventor named Henri Coanda (1886–1972) built an aircraft that was pushed along by a jet of gas. However, it worked in a different way to modern jet engines, and so few people recognize Coanda as the inventor of jet aircraft (although in 2010 Romanians celebrated 100 years of jet travel in their countryman's honor). Coanda's jet used a piston engine to spin a fan inside, which drew air in the front and pushed it out the back, creating thrust. Coanda's aircraft never flew. It caught fire on the runway during its first takeoff. However, his "motor-jet" was used in other ways, powering a sled built for Grand Duke Cyril of Russia. Coanda is better remembered for describing the Coanda Effect, in which liquids are attracted to nearby solid surfaces, a crucial insight that helps explain how airfoils work.

The motor-jet propulsion system using a piston engine and a fan was positioned at the front of the Coanda-1910 biplane.

Grand Duke Cyril in his unique jet-powered motor sled (based on Coanda's design) in 1910.

powered for future conflicts. However, with the economies of so many postwar European countries in tatters, it was left to the United States to lead the way in developing aircraft-engine technology.

The early jet designs were far from perfect, and there were many variations on Whittle's relatively simple design. One of the first improvements made to the jet engine was the inclusion of an afterburner. In Whittle's original engine less than a third of the air drawn in at the front was actually used to burn fuel in the combustion chamber. The remaining air passed out of the rear of the engine with the rest of the exhaust gases. By injecting more fuel into the hot exhaust gases, it was possible to gain a 40 percent increase in the amount of thrust produced by the engine on takeoff. Once the airplane was in the air and traveling at speed, the improvement in thrust was much greater.

It had long been one of the goals of aviation engineers the world over to smash through the invisible obstacle known as the sound barrier. Nevertheless, smashing through

FRANK WHITTLE

In 1928 a young cadet at the Royal Air Force College in Cranwell, England, put forward the idea of replacing the traditional piston-powered engine with a new power source called a turbojet. The cadet, Frank Whittle, had realized that there would soon be a demand for an airplane that could fly much faster than the speed that was possible using a propeller. Whittle submitted plans to the college in which he set out his ideas for a jet-propelled airplane. Unfortunately, Whittle's work was dismissed by the British government. Whittle, however, was convinced that he was on the right track, and his perseverance paid off.

Frank Whittle is commemorated by this statue.

A German Me-262, codenamed the "swallow," was one of the few makes of jet aircraft to fly in World War II. It came into service too late to stop the Allied bombing of Germany.

A ramjet engine, fitted to a P-61 fighter aircraft, being tested in 1947. Ramjets work by using the forward speed of the aircraft to compress the air that mixes with the fuel inside the engine.

CHUCK YEAGER

Yeager was assigned to the U.S. Army Air Corps after enlisting in 1941. He became an outstanding fighter pilot during World War II, flying 64 missions and shooting down a record-breaking four German fighter planes in a single dogfight. After the war, Yeager served briefly as a flight instructor before taking on the far more challenging role of test pilot. When the Bell Company requested a volunteer to act as test pilot for its secret new project, the X-1, Yeager jumped at his chance to make history, even though many fine pilots had already lost their lives trying to break the sound barrier.

this invisible barrier became the goal of the engineers at the American Bell Aircraft Company. All they needed was a highly sophisticated craft and someone brave enough, skilled enough, and foolhardy enough to fly it. This person was Captain Charles "Chuck" Yeager (b. 1923).

Flying the X-1

The X-1 was an unusual airplane. It was essentially a small rocket equipped with four combustion chambers that could be fired independently. The airplane had to be "towed" up into the air strapped underneath a Boeing B-29 bomber. The plan was that at around 30,000 ft (9,100 m) the X-1 would be dropped from the B-29, and Yeager would fire the first of the rocket chambers. In practice this resulted in more than a few difficult moments as Yeager struggled to gain control.

On a crystal clear October 14, 1947, Yeager punched in the rocket engines of the X-1 over Rogers Dry Lake, southern California, and went on to earn himself a well-deserved place in history as the first person ever to fly faster than the speed of sound. In thin air at 43,000 ft (13,100 m) Yeager smashed through the sound barrier at 662 mph (1,066 km/h).

HOW A JET ENGINE WORKS

Jet engines draw in air at the front of the engine. This air is then squeezed and put under pressure by a device called a compressor. Fuel is added to the compressed air and the resulting mixture is ignited in a part of the engine called the combustion chamber. The fuel burns into a mixture of gases, releasing heat—temperatures inside rise to around 700°F (370°C). The heat makes the exhaust gases expand rapidly. This hot, fast-moving exhaust flows out of the back of the engine after first passing through a turbine (which is there to drive fuel pumps, electricity generators, and the compressor at the front of the engine). Jet engines are placed under the wings of the airplane or inside the rear part of the main body (fuselage), with the exhaust gases exiting from beneath the tail.

The way a jet engine works had been described centuries before. In the 17th century, English physicist Isaac Newton (1642–1727) drew up three laws of motion. The third law states that for every action there is an equal and opposite reaction. This means that when hot exhaust gases are ejected at speed from the rear of a jet engine, the resulting opposite force drives the engine—and anything attached to it—forward.

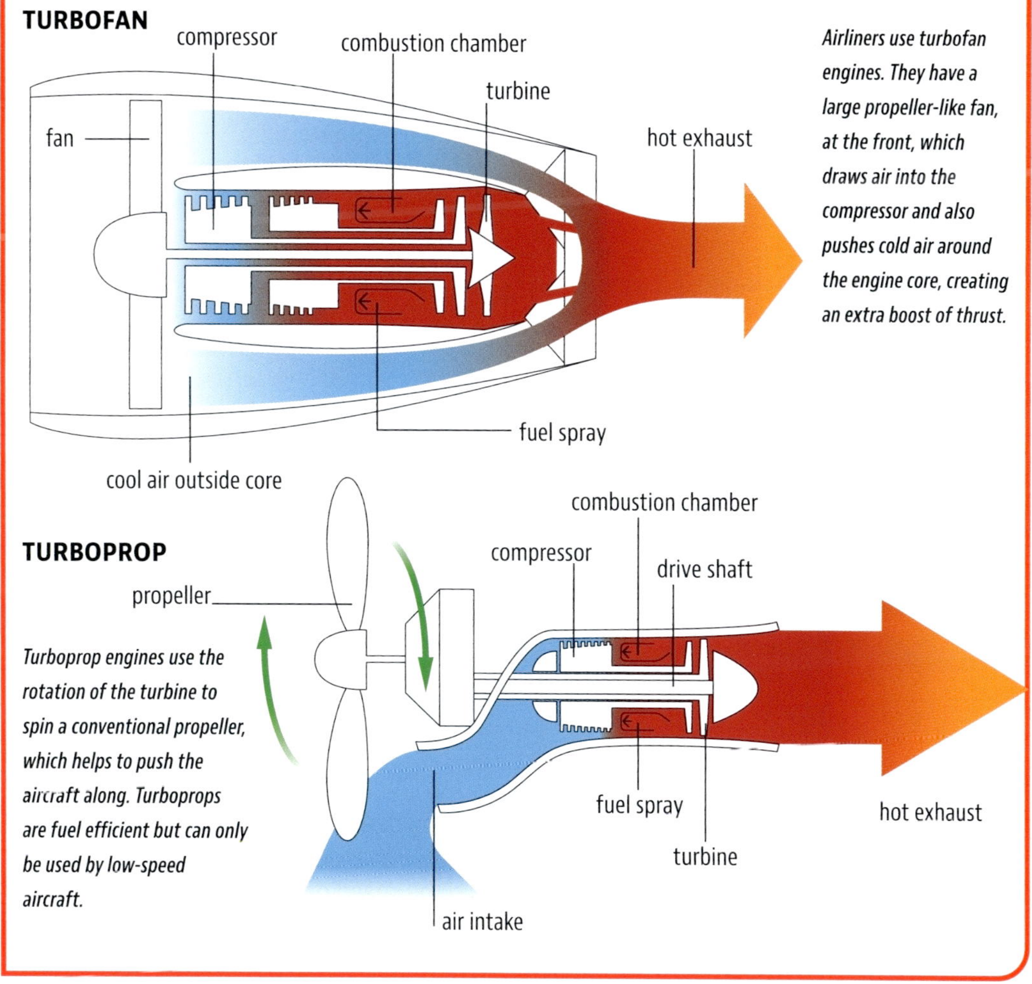

Airliners use turbofan engines. They have a large propeller-like fan, at the front, which draws air into the compressor and also pushes cold air around the engine core, creating an extra boost of thrust.

Turboprop engines use the rotation of the turbine to spin a conventional propeller, which helps to push the aircraft along. Turboprops are fuel efficient but can only be used by low-speed aircraft.

FASTER THAN SOUND

The speed of sound varies according to air pressure. At 40,000 ft (12,100 m), where the air is not very dense, the speed of sound, or Mach 1, is 657 mph (1,060 km/h):

1 When an airplane flies slower than the speed of sound, the pressure waves it makes travel at Mach 1 and radiate in front and behind the plane.
2 When an airplane reaches Mach 1, the air flowing over its surfaces begins to form shock waves as the plane catches up with its own pressure waves. With these shock waves comes an incredible degree of turbulence.
3 As the aircraft moves into supersonic speeds (above Mach 1), the shock waves form a cone that causes a sonic boom to be heard for many miles around as it makes contact with the ground.

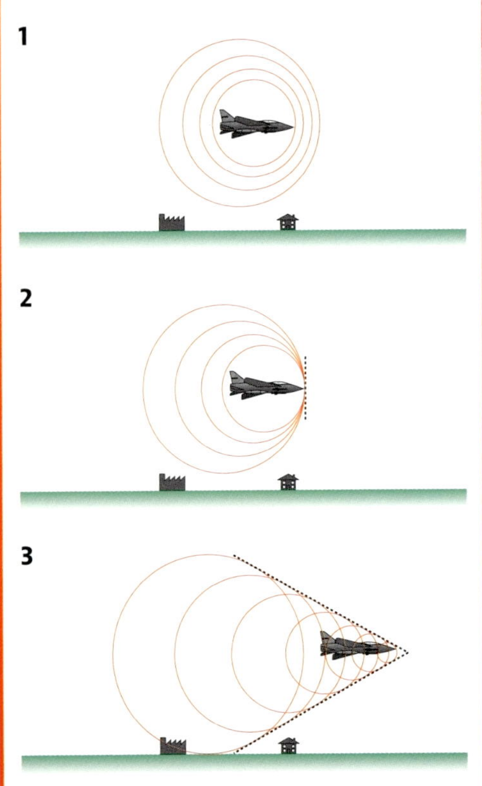

The Bell X-1 design was a "bullet with wings," built to punch through shock waves at the speed of sound.

Capacity and Speed

Today, many military aircraft can travel faster than the speed of sound. The aim of the civilian jet designers, however, has been to build ever larger aircraft capable of carrying the greatest number of fare-paying passengers over long distances for the least possible cost. On the whole, civilian airplane manufacturers have not been particularly interested in getting passengers to their destinations in the shortest possible time. Among designers of military airplanes, however, especially those producing fighters, speed and maneuverability are of the essence.

By the end of the Korean War (1950–1953), military aircraft manufacturers were making highly effective jet-powered fighters. Two notable examples, which met in battle over Korea, were the U.S. Air Force's F-86 Sabre and the former Soviet Union's MiG-15, which the Russians supplied to Korea.

Today's fast military jets employ the "turbojet" engine similar to Whittle's original design, but most civilian aircraft use the turbofan, which is a more efficient engine fitted with a large fan at the front end. This fan drives air around the engine to give

HELICOPTERS

Before the beginning of the 20th century, the helicopter was merely a fascinating concept waiting for engines light enough and powerful enough to make it a reality. A helicopter is a flying machine that creates lift with a spinning wing, or rotor. Airfoils create lift by air rushing around them at high speed. Fixed wings do this by powering down a runway, while a helicopter's spinning rotor rushes through the air with the rest of the aircraft remaining still. This method allows helicopters to rise straight up into the air from a small pad, rather than a long runway, and hover in one place in the air.

The earliest known reference to a rotor-powered flying machine appears in a Chinese text dated 320 CE. It was not until 1907, however, that the very first piloted helicopter lifted off (although that was all it did, being capable only of vertical motion). In 1939 the first practical—and steerable—helicopter was introduced, in the United States, by Russian-born engineer Igor Sikorsky (1889–1972; see inset picture, below). In the 1950s, engineers adapted the jet engine for use in helicopters, enabling them to travel farther and faster. Helicopters were used in the Korean War, but became truly practical warplanes in the Vietnam War (1957–1975). Bell UH-1 transport helicopters (or "Hueys") were used to carry troops, while other helicopters were used as strike aircraft.

The ability of a helicopter to hover in the air makes it a useful flying machine. Rescue helicopters equipped with winches are the fastest way to get people away from danger.

VERTICAL TAKEOFF AND LANDING

The classic Harrier "jump jets" have swiveling exhaust outlets that direct thrust down as well as backward.

V/STOL AIRCRAFT

Speed was not the only consideration when designing new aircraft. In 1954, the U.S. Navy developed the Convair XFY-1, the world's first plane that could perform a vertical takeoff. Known as the Pogo Stick, the XFY-1 stood on its tail while on the ground and took off straight up using propellers at the tip of the nose. In the air, the aircraft flew normally, but rotated upright again to land, slowly dropping on to its tail.

The Pogo Stick design was difficult to fly. A better Vertical/Short TakeOff and Landing (V/STOL) plane was the Harrier "jump jet." A Harrier was powered by two compact jet engines. During normal flight the jets pointed backward, but they could swivel to point downward. A more recent V/STOL is the F-35B Lightning, which entered service in 2015. This uses a rotating nozzle from its rear engine to land in confined areas, with support from three other less powerful nozzles to balance it and enable it to make use of small runways or to land on ships.

increased thrust—but limits the aircraft to subsonic speeds. Other types of jet include the turboprop engine—a jet turbine that turns a propeller—and the turboshaft, which is similar to the turboprop but is used to drive the rotors of a helicopter.

Stealth Planes

As well as developing faster, more maneuverable aircraft, military designers need to make their planes harder for the enemy to locate. The result is "stealth" technology, a project initially set up by the United States government and Lockheed in 1980, and now

SCIENCE WORDS

Altitude: The height above sea level.
Combustion: When a substance burns.
Supersonic: Faster than sound.
Turbine: A series of propellers or fans that spin around when gases—or liquids—flow over them.

V-22 OSPREY: HALF PLANE, HALF HELICOPTER

1 The aircraft's rotors point upward for a vertical takeoff.

2 Once in the air, the pilot swivels the rotors around.

3 The rotors are positioned facing front, and the Osprey flies forward like other airplanes.

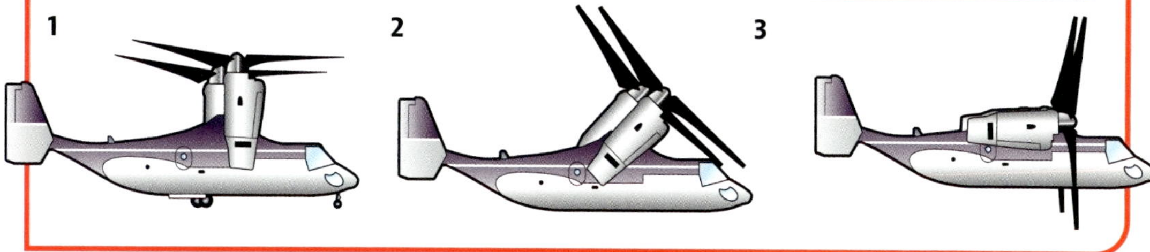

SOCIETY AND INVENTIONS

Airliners in the Jet Age

As economies began to recover, following World War II, aircraft manufacturers looked to the growing market in international air travel as the way forward. The British aircraft industry decided to concentrate on the production of innovative civilian passenger aircraft. Unable to compete against the mighty piston-engined airplanes from American companies Lockheed and Douglas, such as the DC-7, British companies began to look at the possibility of fitting a jet engine to a passenger airplane. In 1952 the British-based company de Havilland introduced the de Havilland Comet, the first jet airliner. In 1958, Boeing introduced the 707, the first purpose-built jet airliner. Within 20 years, jet-powered air travel was within the reach of millions, making widespread, affordable air travel possible for more people than ever before. By the late 20th century, it seemed the Jet Age would involve ever-faster travel. Luxurious supersonic planes, such as Concorde (introduced in 1976), dramatically cut the time taken for transatlantic flights but proved far too expensive to run. Low-cost, short-haul flights became increasingly popular instead. In the 21st century, airplane designers are switching attention to making planes quieter and more environmentally friendly, using less-polluting fuels such as hydrogen and, in the future, perhaps even completely electric power.

The largest passenger jet in service is the A380 "superjumbo." Up to 850 passenger seats are arranged over two decks. The giant aircraft can fly 9,400 miles (15,200 km) without stops.

SUPERSONIC CONCORDE

While most military planes are supersonic, few civilian planes have been manufactured that can travel faster than the speed of sound. In 1976, the first and only passenger-carrying supersonic airliner came into service. Concorde was the result of a joint project between Britain and France. However, the fleet of 16 Concordes were expensive to operate and they were banned from many airports because of the loud sonic booms they created. In 2001, a Concorde crashed soon after takeoff in Paris, killing everyone on board. The other 15 planes were passed safe to continue flying, but the fleet was finally retired in 2003.

used in all fields of military design, not just aircraft. Stealth aircraft are extremely difficult to detect using radar. This means that the aircraft need not be as fast or as maneuverable as other kinds of combat aircraft, since they are seldom attacked. This makes them ideal for surprise attacks.

The first stealth fighter was the Lockheed F-117 Nighthawk, a single-seater plane unveiled in 1983. Two other fighters used by the U.S. Air Force, the F-22 Raptor, and the F-35 Lightning, are also stealth aircraft. It is said that the twin-engine Raptor shows up as the size of a marble when scanned by radar, while the Lightning is easier to see—it's radar echo is the same size as one produced by a golf ball. "Stealth" uses a combination of technologies. The jagged shape, low profile, and use of dark, iron ball paint to absorb radar energy make stealth planes hard to detect in flight.

The B-2 Spirit, also known as the "stealth bomber," has a "flying wing" design. At a cost of $1billion per plane, the B-2 is the most expensive aircraft ever built.

STEALTH PLANE

The shape of the Lockheed F-117 Nighthawk was kept a secret by the United States government until 1988. It was designed to be virtually undetectable by radar—especially at night and in cloudy weather. While the surfaces of normal airplanes are smooth and rounded for aerodynamic reasons, the surfaces of the F-117 are highly faceted (have many faces). Even the edges of the cockpit are jagged. This ensures that enemy radar is harmlessly deflected in several directions rather than being reflected back to the enemy in a recognizable pattern. The engine air inlets are covered by grids to confuse enemy radar, and the jet nozzles are wide and flat so that the hot exhaust gases are spread out as they leave, making less of a target for heatseeking missiles. Low detectability was achieved, however, at the expense of aerodynamics, speed, and maneuverability, making the F-117 a difficult plane to fly. It has a digital control center to make steering easier, but pilots have still dubbed it the "wobbly goblin." The main advantage of the F-117 is in its ability to sneak up on a target (albeit slowly), take pictures or film, and launch a guided missile or "smart" bomb. However, the stealth plane is not immune to attack. In 1999, an F-117 was shot down over Serbia by a missile targeted by human spotters on the ground.

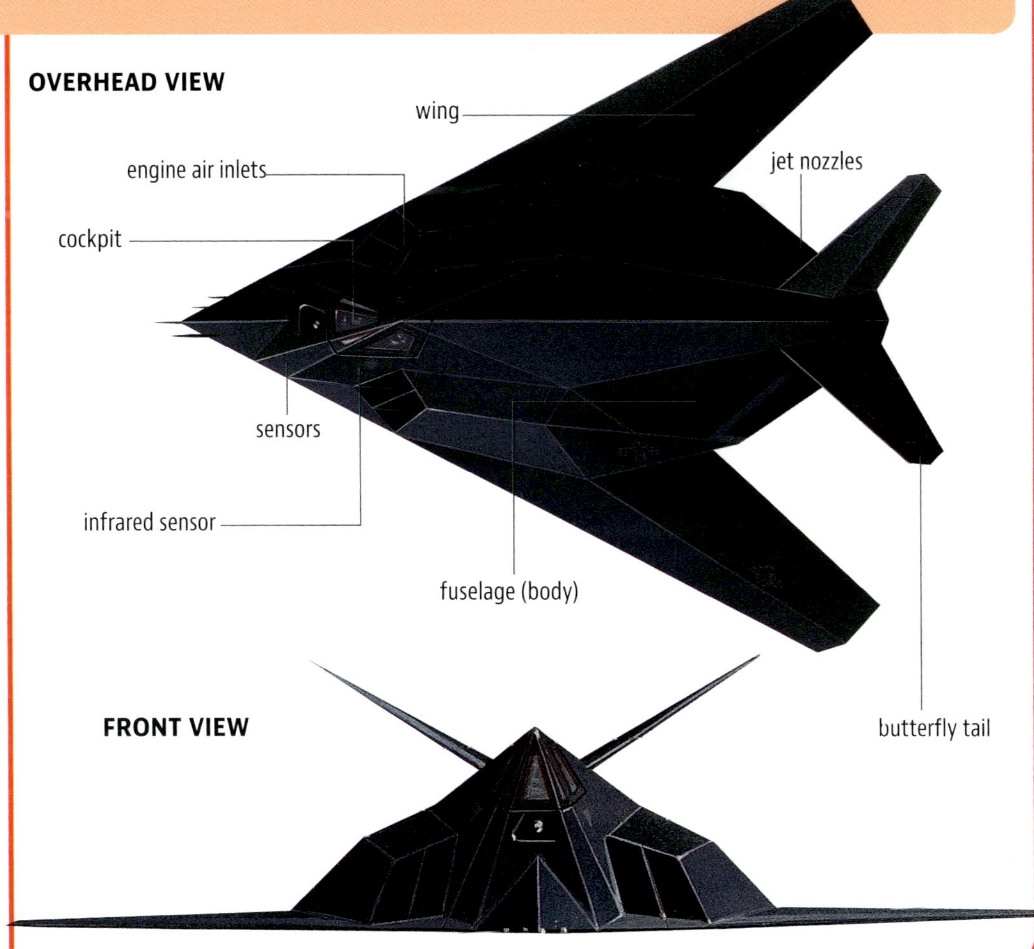

FACTS AND FIGURES

- The Bell X-1 had a single rocket engine, a maximum speed of 949 mph (1,531 km/h), and a wingspan of 28 ft (8.5 m).
- Concorde had four turbojet engines, a maximum speed of 1,380 mph (2,226 km/h), and a wingspan of 84 ft (25.6 m).
- Lockheed's F-117 Nighthawk (stealth fighter) has two turbofan (jet) engines, a maximum speed of 641 mph (1,034 km/h), and a wingspan of 43 ft (13 m).

Beyond the Range of Attack

Another method of aircraft defense is not to avoid detection, but to be beyond the range of weapons sent to attack. The Lockheed SR-71 Blackbird was a spyplane that operated between the 1970s and 2000s. It could fly faster than Mach 3 and went so high that the pilot wore something similar to a spacesuit. The Blackbird holds the record for the fastest jet aircraft (2,193.2 mph; 3,529.6 km/h). If this plane was detected by an enemy, the pilot could easily outrun any surface-to-air missile launched to destroy it. Today's spy planes are pilotless "drones" that are easy to replace if destroyed and so do not need to fly fast or high.

An MQ-1 Predator is a pilotless "drone" aircraft powered by a propeller. Drones are used to spy on the enemy and to fire weapons at ground targets by remote control.

Future Developments

With the success of slow reconnaissance and ground attack "drones," a key development in military aviation is likely to be high-performance robot aircraft, piloted from a control room on the ground, taking part in air battles of the future. Civilian aircraft will use ever more lightweight materials in place of metal bodies to save on fuel, as airliners get bigger and fly for longer.

MODERN STRIKE AIRCRAFT

The F-35 Lightning was the latest fighter jet developed for the American and British military. The first jets went into service in 2015.

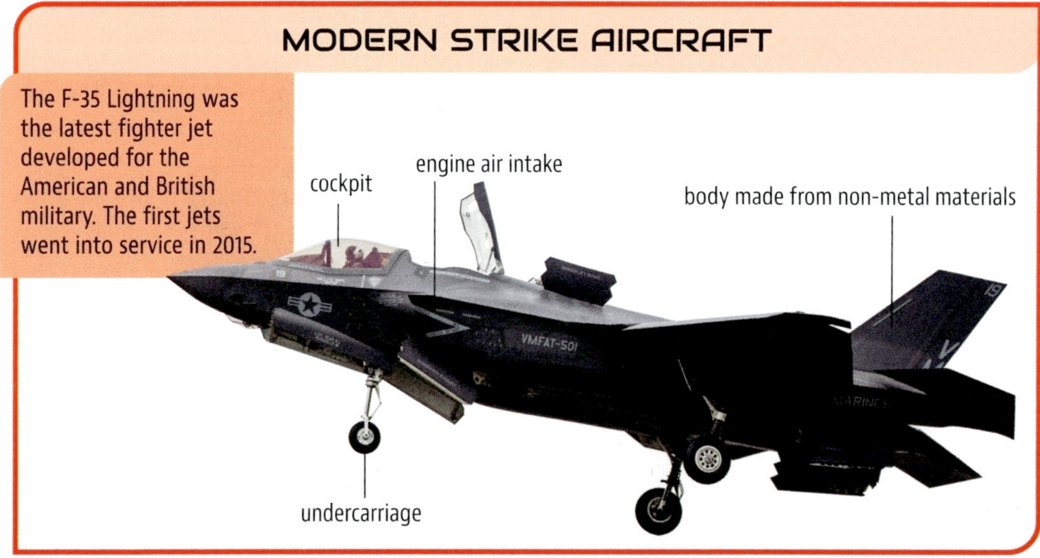

COMBAT HELICOPTER

The helicopter shown here is the AH-64 Apache made by Boeing. It is an attack helicopter used by the U.S. military and several other countries. The Apache is designed to operate above battlefields and needs to be fast but also highly maneuverable. It shares certain structural features with most helicopters. The tail and main rotor assemblies, which are driven by a turboshaft jet engine, are used to produce lift. Each rotor blade becomes an airfoil (a curved "wing" shape that generates lift). As the blades spin around, a huge volume of air is thrown downward and this pushes the helicopter upward. Hinges in the rotor hub allow the pilot to alter each main rotor blade's pitch (angle) so that the craft can be steered. For example, increasing the pitch of the blades as they pass over the helicopter's nose makes the craft fly backward. This particular helicopter has a tailwheel; others have inflatable floats for landing on water or skis for touching down on rough or soft ground.

The Apache has room for a pilot and a gunner in the cockpit. The weapons are targeted using a system linked to the gunner's helmet. Wherever the gunner looks, the laser guidance system follows, so missiles can hit whatever the crew can see.

The Apache helicopter entered service in 1986. It has two engines, one mounted on either side of the aircraft. If one engine is damaged, the other is powerful enough to fly the helicopter to a safe landing area.

THE SPACE AGE

The story of flight does not end at the edge of Earth's atmosphere. Spacecraft can leave the planet behind and fly in space. However, without any air to create lift, spaceflight required new technologies.

Spacecraft are powered by rockets. Only rockets work outside Earth's atmosphere because, unlike most other types of engine, they do not require oxygen from the air to burn their fuel.

The Chinese were using rockets as weapons as early as the 13th century, and rockets soon reached the Arab world. In the West, rockets were used most widely as fireworks, although they were use as weapons for a short time by British artillery officer William Congreve (1772–1828).

CONQUERING GRAVITY

The greatest barrier to space travel and flight in general has always been gravity. This is a force that attracts objects toward one another. The law of gravity, discovered by English physicist Isaac Newton (1643–1727), states that the strength of the force is determined by the mass of the two objects and the distance that separates them. When an object is released in midair, gravity pulls it back toward Earth. In order to remain airborne, an aircraft or spacecraft must produce an upward force (lift) greater than the downward force of gravity—but aircraft wings and engines will not work outside the atmosphere. At present, the only engine powerful enough to leave Earth and to operate in the vacuum of space is the rocket.

Fireworks, simple types of rockets invented in China, explode above Shanghai's Huangpu River.

The launch of Long March 3B Rocket, Xichang Satellite Center, China, in 1996. It is mainly used to put communications satellites into orbit.

TSIOLKOVSKY

Konstantin Tsiolkovsky, a Russian schoolteacher, was the first person to suggest using rockets to fly into space. He even proposed a liquid-fuel rocket powered by super-chilled liquid hydrogen and liquid oxygen—these are fuels used by the largest rockets today.

Tsiolkovsky also invented the multistage rocket, which he called a "rocket train." To reach space, a rocket has to carry large amounts of fuel, but the larger the rocket, the more it weighs, and the more empty weight it will be dragging with it as it reaches space. Multistage rockets have several segments of decreasing size. Each stage has its own liquid-fuel tanks and engine. The first and largest stage supplies the thrust to get the rocket off the ground, sometimes helped by solid- or liquid-fuel boosters.

As the fuel in these early stages is exhausted, the stages are separated from the rest of the vehicle (jettisoned) and fall back to Earth. The rocket engines on the next stage then fire to carry the now lighter rocket farther into space. The upper stages carry less fuel than the first stage, but they accelerate the vehicle quickly, because they are pushing a reduced weight.

It was not until the 1890s that someone had the idea of using rockets in space. Encouraged by the theories of Russian Konstantin Tsiolkovsky (1857–1935) and others, many scientists became interested in rockets in the early 20th century. American physics professor Robert Hutchings Goddard (1882–1945) was one such pioneer. He built the first practical liquid-fuel rockets and set many altitude records for rockets. During World War II (1939–1945) he worked on military uses for his rockets, but his designs were never put into service.

World War II

Germany had a highly successful rocket program throughout World War II. It was led by Wernher von Braun (1912–1977), who had been studying rocketry on a team led by German physics professor and rocket pioneer Hermann Oberth (1894–1989) since 1930. Von Braun's first rockets, the bomb-carrying V-2s, were launched at Britain, France, and Holland by Germany during the war, but did not alter the outcome.

Sergei Korolev (1906–1966) was the great Russian pioneer of practical rocketry. In 1932, he became director of the Moscow Group Studying the Principles of Propulsion by Rocket Engines, and launched the Soviet Union's (USSR's) first rocket the following year.

On October 4, 1957, the USSR (a large communist state, now broken up, centered on

EARLY ROCKET DESIGNS

1 Tsiolkovsky's first spaceship design of 1903 envisaged the use of liquid hydrogen as fuel, and liquid oxygen as the oxidant, which provides the oxygen to burn the fuel. It also included exhaust vanes to steer the rocket by controlling the direction of the thrust.

2 A crewed rocket was designed by Tsiolkovsky in 1911 in which the passenger lay face-upward on the floor of the top section. Today's rocket scientists have figured out that the curved combustion chamber in this design would have severely reduced the rocket's performance.

3 Tsiolkovsky's rocket design of 1915 shows details of the valves that control the flow of fuel and oxidant into the combustion chamber. This design first appeared on the cover of Tsiolkovsky's book *Dreams of Earth and Sky* (1935).

4 The first liquid-fuel rocket to actually fly was designed by American Robert Goddard in 1926. It used liquid oxygen as the oxidant and gasoline as the fuel.

5 The "cone motor," designed by German engineer Hermann Oberth in 1929 and 1930, also burned liquid oxygen and gasoline. This simple rocket was widely used in German rocket experiments of the 1930s.

6 Oberth's "Modell B" design, a two-stage rocket, was never built, but many of its features are incorporated in modern multistage rockets. The first stage uses liquid oxygen and alcohol as propellants, while the second stage uses liquid oxygen and liquid hydrogen as propellants. Modell B also had stabilizing fins to prevent the rocket from spinning in the air (this would have caused it to fly out of control).

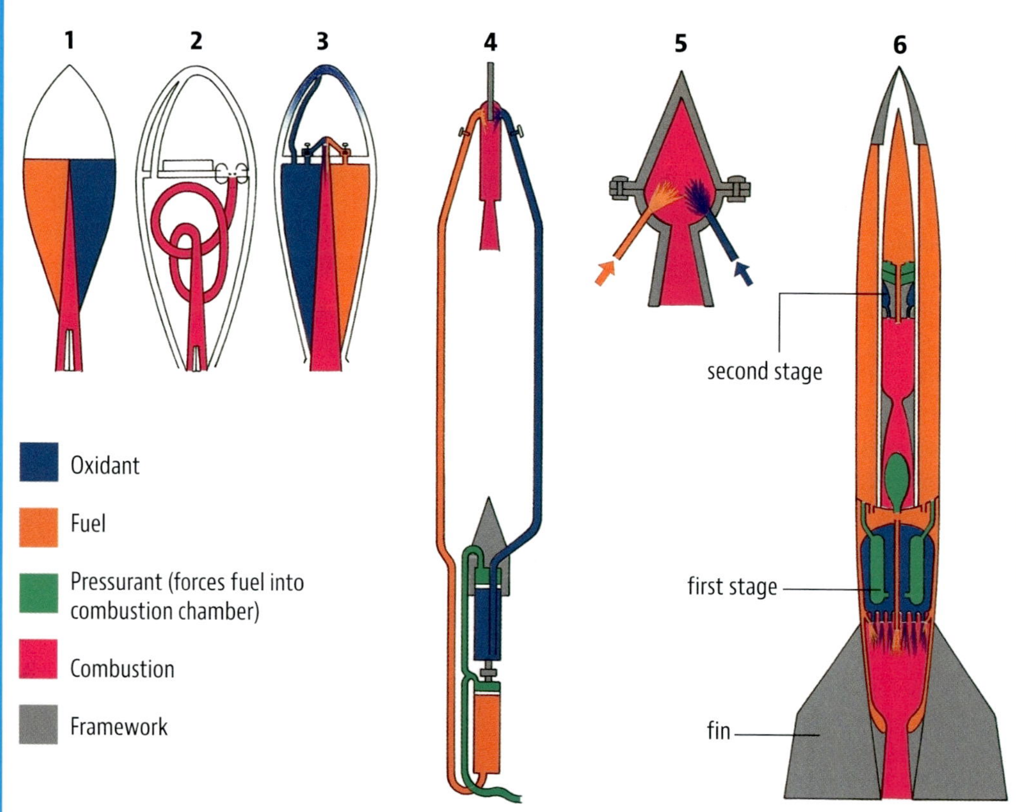

what is now Russia) stunned the world by announcing the successful launch of the satellite Sputnik 1. Radio listeners all over the world could pick up its distinctive "beep-beep" as it orbited Earth. The U.S. Army launched its first successful satellite, Explorer 1, in January 1958. Later that year, the National Aeronautics and Space Administration (NASA) was founded to coordinate the United States' civilian space program.

Today, there are many types of satellite in orbit. Communications satellites orbit farthest out, acting as relays for telephone calls, TV signals, and other information beamed around the world. Closer to Earth, space becomes more crowded. Remote-sensing satellites study Earth from space, monitoring weather, searching for minerals, or spying on other countries. They orbit at altitudes of up to 625 miles (1,000 km), usually in polar orbits.

HOW ROCKETS WORK

Newton's third law of motion states that for every action there is an equal and opposite reaction. Rocket engines provide thrust using this principle. Substances (propellants) that move the rocket are burned in the combustion chamber, and the resulting hot exhaust gases escape through the cone-shaped nozzle at high speed. This action provides a force that propels the rocket in the opposite direction (the reaction).

Rockets need two types of propellant: a fuel source and an oxidant, which provides oxygen so that the fuel can burn. Solid-fuel rockets usually consist of a metal cylinder packed with propellants and a nozzle at one end to let gases escape. The cylinder acts as the combustion chamber. Liquid-fuel rockets are more complex but easier to control. The fuel (often liquid hydrogen) and the oxidant (liquid oxygen) are stored in separate tanks and pumped into the combustion chamber by separate pumps. There the propellants are ignited, and the hot exhaust gases escape through the nozzle at the rocket's base.

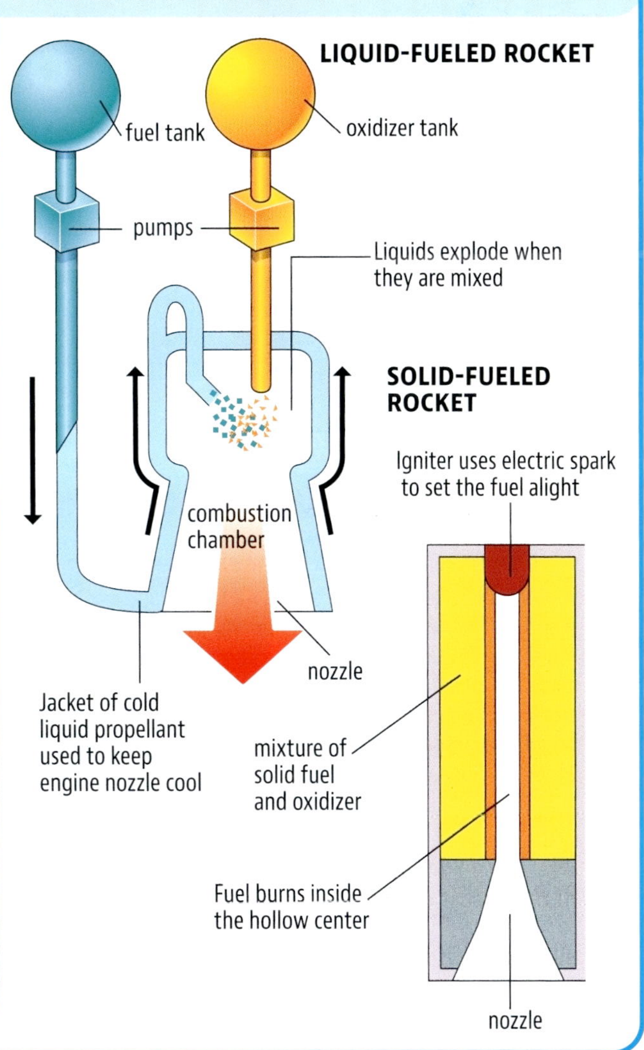

ARTIFICIAL SATELLITES

A satellite is an object that orbits a planet, held in place by the planet's gravitational field. The Moon is a natural satellite. Artificial satellites do not have to be aerodynamic and can be any shape.

1 The first artificial satellite, Sputnik 1, provided data on temperature and density in the upper atmosphere. Launched by the Soviet Union on October 4, 1957, it weighed 185 lb (84 kg). It flew around Earth in a low orbit 1,440 times.

2 Explorer 1 was the first successful U.S. satellite. It allowed scientists to discover that Earth is girdled by bands of radiation held in place by the planet's magnetic field. Weighing 31 lb (14 kg), Explorer 1 was launched on January 31, 1958.

3 Sputnik 2 carried a dog, Laika, to study the effects of orbital flight. Her heart rate and other signs of life were measured. Sputnik 2, launched on November 3, 1957, weighed 1,120 lb (508 kg).

4 Currently, small satellites using nanotechnology and weighing just 2.2 to 22 lb (1 to 10 kg) are being launched in groups called "swarms."

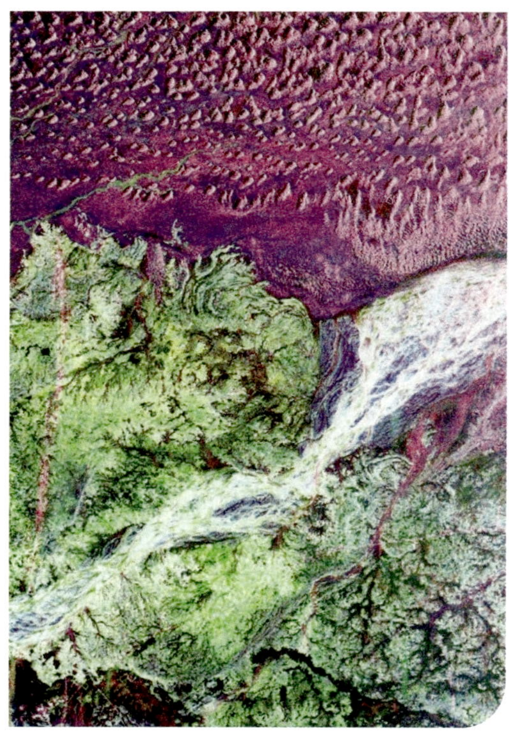

A satellite radar image of the Arabian desert shows up features that are hard to see from the ground. The image has been colored to show areas of rock (green), riverbed (white), and sand (blue and purple).

GLOBAL POSITIONING SYSTEM

The Earth is surrounded by a network of Navstar satellites 12,552 miles (20,200 km) up. These satellites are a part of the Global Positioning System (GPS). A GPS navigation device picks up different Navstar signals and uses them to work out the positions of each satellite. From that, the GPS device figures out its exact position to within a few feet. GPS is an American system: other countries have their own networks, such as China's Beidou system.

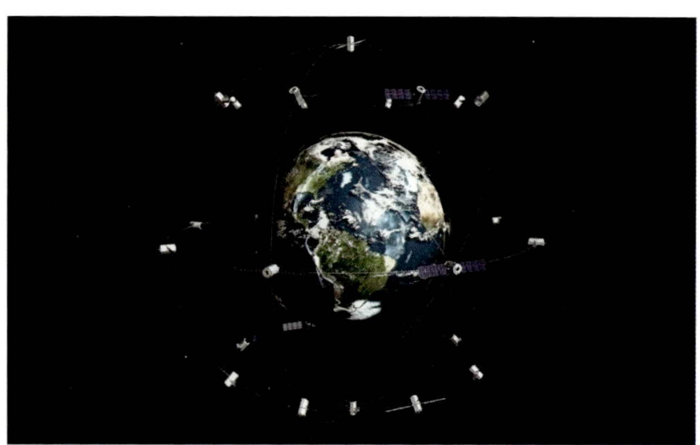

The constellation of Navstar satellites orbit Earth. GPS devices need to receive data from four satellites to function.

EARTH ORBITS

Low Earth Orbits (LEOs), which are between 190 and 250 miles (300 and 400 km) up and parallel to Earth's equator, are the easiest orbits to achieve because the rocket picks up extra speed from Earth's own rotation. Satellites in this orbit circle Earth in about 90 minutes.

Elliptical orbits are shaped like stretched circles, or pointed ovals. The satellite passes close to Earth at one point and travels much farther out into space at another. Scientific satellites often use this type of orbit so that they can gather information on the conditions in space at the farthest point of their orbits without interference from Earth.

Polar orbits are orbits that pass over or near the poles. This type of orbit allows satellites to survey most of the surface of Earth as it rotates under them. But achieving this type of orbit needs a more powerful rocket than needed to put a satellite in Low Earth Orbit.

The geostationary orbit was worked out in 1945 by British science-fiction writer Arthur C. Clarke (1917–2008). This is the orbit 22,300 miles (35,900 km) above the equator in which a satellite circles Earth in precisely one day, always remaining above the same place on Earth. Weather, communication, and broadcasting satellites often have geostationary orbits.

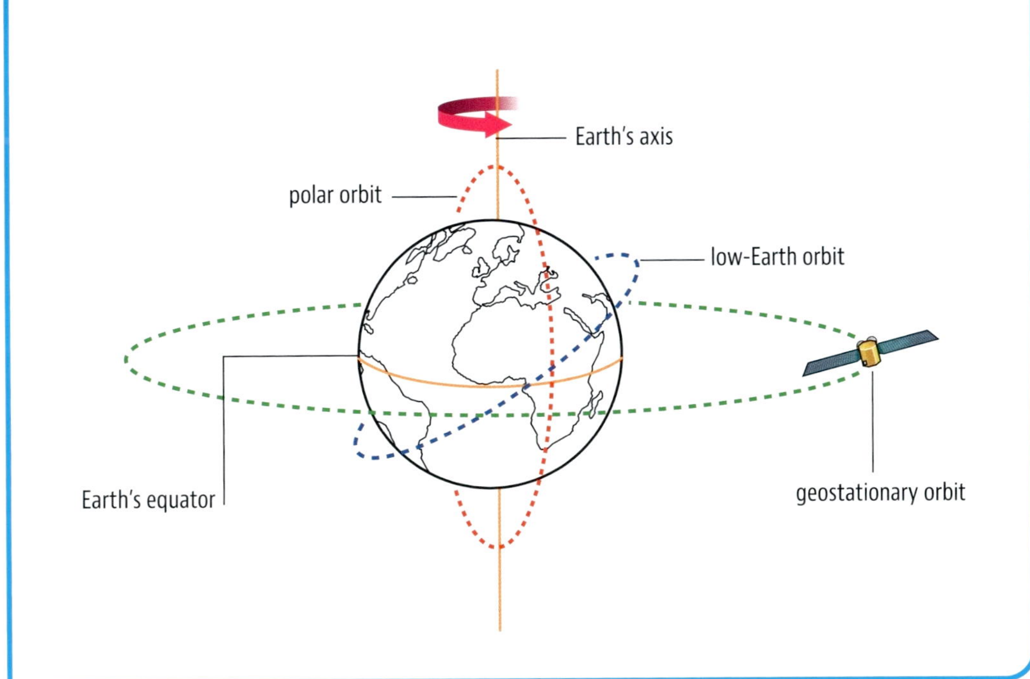

Humans in Space

As well as launching machines into orbit, scientists sent people to explore space. Sealed capsules with air supplies were first tested on animals, proving that living things could return from orbit alive. The next step was to put a person in space.

In 1961, the first human spaceflight was made by Yuri Gagarin (1934–1968) in the Soviet *Vostock 1* spacecraft. Throughout the following decade, crewed spaceflights became longer and more ambitious. The American Gemini missions carried two men into space, sometimes staying in orbit for several days,

SPACE FIRSTS

In 1961, the first crewed spacecraft, the Soviet Union's *Vostok 1*, orbited Earth with Yuri Gagarin, on board. The craft was controlled by autopilot. The United States followed a few weeks later, putting first Alan Shepard (1923–1998) into space, and then John Glenn (1921–2016). In 1963, Soviet cosmonaut Valentina Tereshkova (b. 1937) become the first woman to travel into space.

Yuri Gagarin prepares to enter his rocket Vostock 1 *in 1961. His two-hour space flight made him an international celebrity.*

and performed the first docking of two spacecraft. The Gemini missions also established how to movefrom one orbit to another by firing its rockets. If they were used to increase the speed, it moved into a higher orbit. If retrorockets were used (these are rockets that fire in the same direction the craft is moving in order to slow it down) the craft then moved into a lower orbit.

Freedom 7 *launched from Cape Canaveral in 1961. Inside the black pod is Alan Shepard. The spacecraft did not go into orbit. It dropped back to Earth after around three minutes in space.*

SPACESUITS

The first spacesuits were modified versions of pressure suits worn by jet pilots, but they were reinvented in the mid-1960s to allow astronauts to leave their spacecraft and "spacewalk." A sealed outer suit made from airtight materials such as Nylon and Teflon provides protection against heat, cold, radiation from the Sun, and tiny space particles called micrometeorites.

Astronauts are often in very low-pressure environments, where the boiling point of the blood is normal body temperature. An inflatable inner layer of the spacesuit maintains a constant pressure on the body to prevent this happening. Excess heat is removed by water circulating in a network of tubes under the main suit. Tough outer layers provide protection, and folds in the material allow for limited movement. The backpack contains the life-support system that allows the astronaut to breathe.

NASA has also developed a rocket-powered suit for flying independently around a spacecraft in an emergency. Back on Earth, outfits similar to spacesuits have been designed for sufferers of rare light-sensitive disorders, enabling them to go outside in daylight for the first time.

Weightlessness

An orbiting spacecraft is, in effect, continuously falling toward Earth, but since it is traveling at such extremely high speeds, the Earth's surface curves away as the craft moves forward. Because both the spacecraft and its contents are continuously moving at the same rate, there appears to be no gravity. This results in the condition that is called weightlessness, microgravity, or zero gravity. Everything inside the spacecraft has to be fixed down or it will float around.

FACTS AND FIGURES

- For a spacecraft to travel farther than Earth's atmosphere and reach orbit, it must be traveling at least 4.9 miles per second (7.8 km/s).
- For a spacecraft to escape Earth's gravity altogether it must reach a velocity (speed) of at least 6.8 miles per second (11 km/s). This is called the escape velocity.

SATURN V

The rocket had three stages, each with its own engines. The launch escape system was a small rocket that could take off separately in case of any mishaps during launch, carrying the three-person crew in the command module to safety.

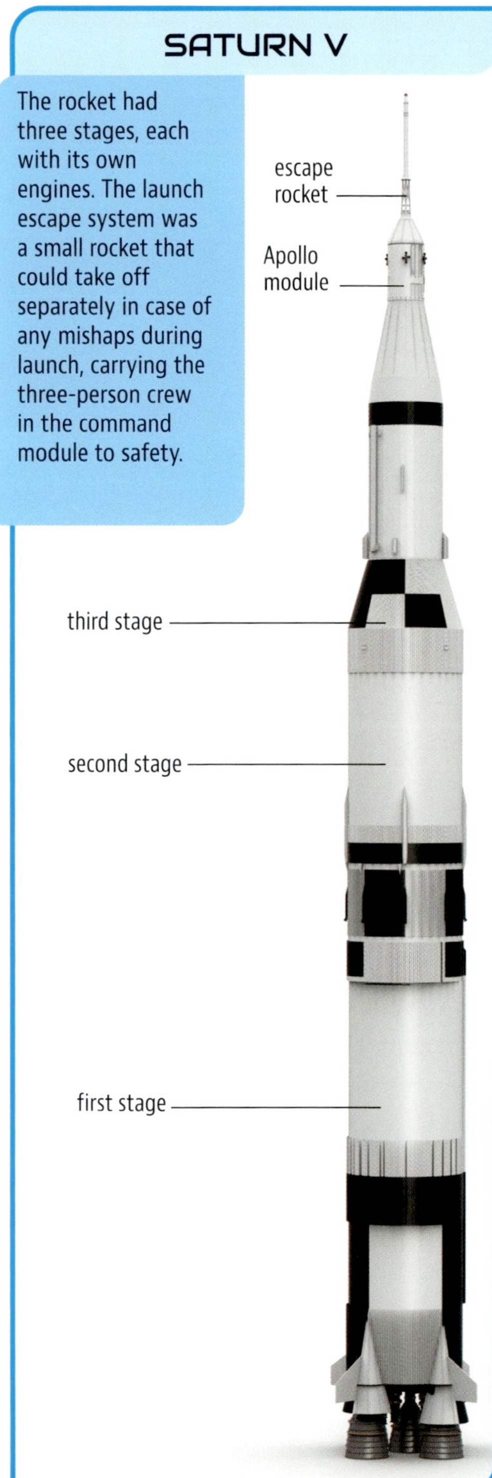

Buzz Aldrin poses for a photograph on the Moon. His crew mate, Neil Armstrong (taking the picture), and the Lunar Module are reflected in Aldrin's mirror visor.

The Race to the Moon

In 1961, U.S. President John F. Kennedy (1917–1963) announced NASA's Apollo Moon Program, which had the goal of putting astronauts on the Moon by 1970.

The Apollo spacecraft had three modules. The command and service modules were designed to just orbit the Moon, from where the lunar module (LM) would separate and fly down to the surface. The Apollo spacecraft were carried into space by a Saturn V rocket.

JOURNEY TO THE MOON

The Apollo missions were among the most complex and ambitious voyages ever. The diagram below shows the main stages of the trip to the Moon:

1 Saturn V lifts off and enters orbit around Earth.

2 The Apollo spacecraft leaves orbit. The command and service module (CSM) separates and links to the lunar module (LM).

3 LM and CSM enter orbit around the Moon using retrorockets, which fire in the same direction of travel, to reduce speed.

4 LM separates and prepares to land. CSM remains in orbit around the Moon.

5 LM uses radar to gauge its height and fires its retrorockets to slow down during its approach. It soft lands on the lunar surface.

6 LM ascent stage lifts off from the Moon and rejoins the CSM in orbit. All astronauts return to the CSM, which separates from the LM, leaving it to crash into the Moon, while the CSM sets a course back to Earth.

7 The command module (CM) separates from the service module, which burns up in the atmosphere, while the CM reenters the atmosphere and makes a safe splashdown in the Pacific Ocean, using parachutes to slow its fall.

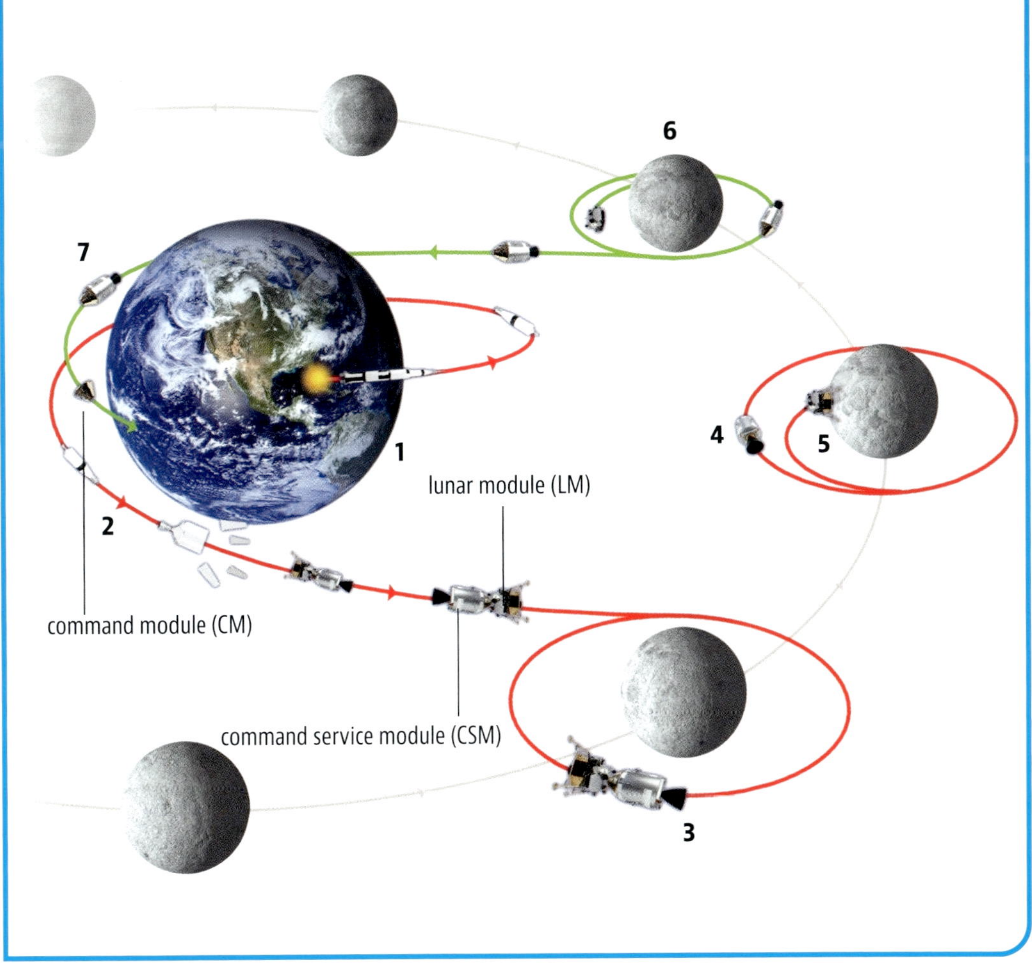

After a series of test runs, the Apollo 11 mission launched in July 16, 1969. On July 20, with the Apollo capsule in orbit around the Moon, astronauts Buzz Aldrin (b. 1930) and Neil Armstrong (1930–2012) boarded the Eagle LM and separated from the orbiter, crewed by Michael Collins (b. 1930). The LM had retrorockets to slow it down, and it made a perfect, soft landing in the "Sea of Tranquility" on the Moon. Neil Armstrong stepped out, becoming the first person on the Moon. In total, 12 Americans, visited the Moon. No one has visited since December 1972, though by there have been almost 60 uncrewed missions to and around the Moon by the United States, Russia, China, and India since then.

The Space Shuttle

The first space shuttle, *Columbia*, was launched in 1981. *Columbia* and four other craft, *Challenger*, *Discovery*, *Atlantis*, and

There were more than 130 space shuttle flights over 30 years of service. The shuttle that flew the most was Discovery, *which made 38 journeys into space.*

SOCIETY AND INVENTIONS

Space Science Applications

Space exploration has sometimes been criticized due to its enormous cost. However, many of the advances made by space scientists and engineers have everyday uses. Many are in the area of medicine. Advanced pacemakers for patients with irregular heartbeats have been developed using NASA's two-way communication technology, first used to communicate with satellites. Doctors can adjust these pacemakers from outside a patient's body, improving the regulation of the heartbeat. Surgical heart pumps based on aerospace engine pump technologies have been developed. Astronauts who spend long periods in space can suffer from weakened hearts and muscles. The Telemedicine Instrumentation Pack (TIP) was used on space shuttle missions to make physical examinations of the crew and send the results to doctors on Earth. A TIP can also be used in remote areas by people with little training to consult with medics in other locations, bringing healthcare to people with no local doctor.

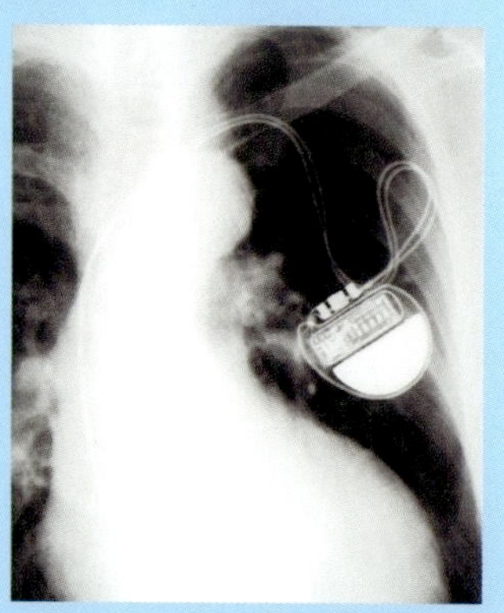

Thanks to space science, modern pacemakers can be fine-tuned by doctors from outside the body.

HOW THE SPACE SHUTTLE FLEW

1 Solid-fuel rocket boosters were strapped to an empty fuel tank on the mobile launch platform at the Vehicle Assembly Building (VAB) of the Kennedy Space Center.
2 The orbiter was attached to the solid rocket boosters (SRBs) and external tank, and the whole structure was then moved to the launch complex.
3 The external tank was filled with liquid hydrogen (bottom segment) and liquid oxygen (top). Takeoff was powered by the two boosters and the orbiter's three main rocket engines.
4 Two minutes after takeoff, at an altitude (height) of 28 miles (45 km), the boosters separated.
5 At an altitude of 68 miles (109 km), before orbit was reached, the main engines cut off and the now-empty external fuel tank separated.
6 Two smaller maneuvering rockets on the orbiter propeled it into the required orbit.
7 On return to Earth, the orbiter reversed its direction and fired main engines to slow the spacecraft down as it reentered the atmosphere.
8 Back in Earth's atmosphere, the orbiter glided like an aircraft and came to land on the runway, at speeds of up to 226 mph (364 km/h).
After checks and repairs, the orbiter could be used again.

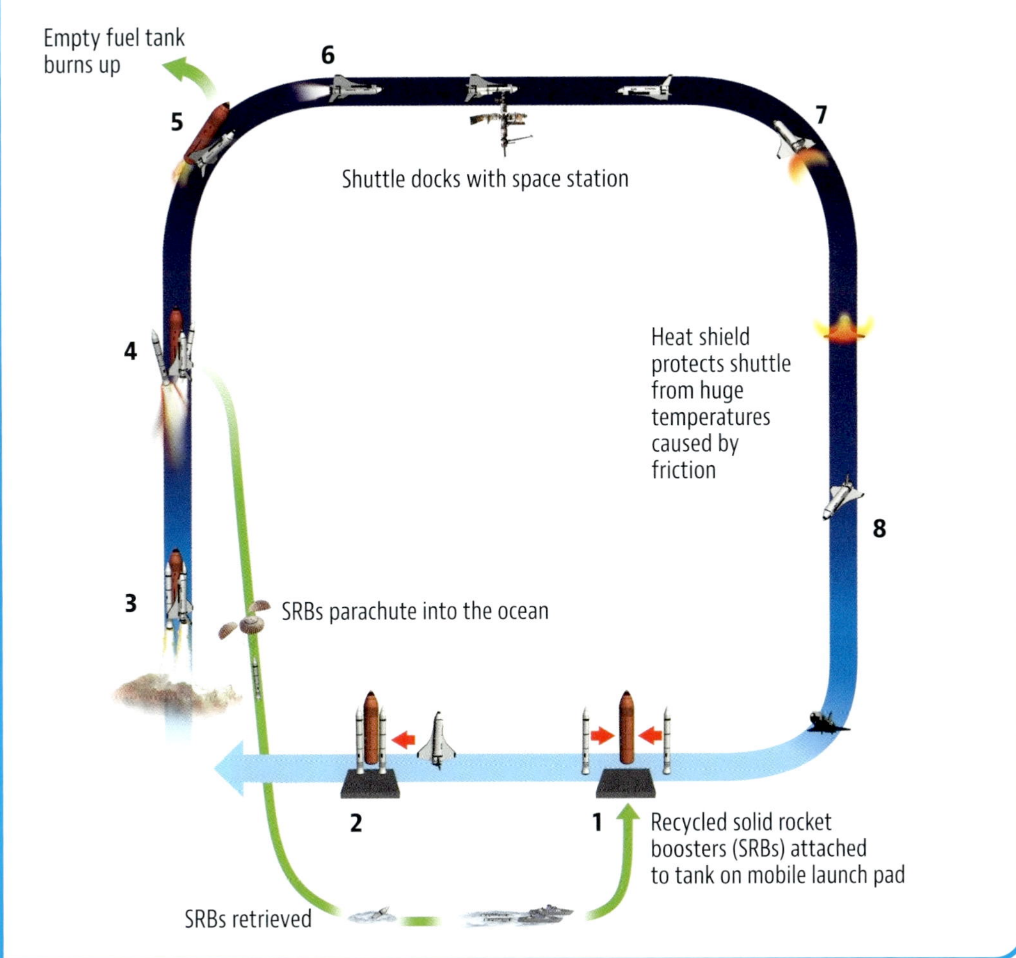

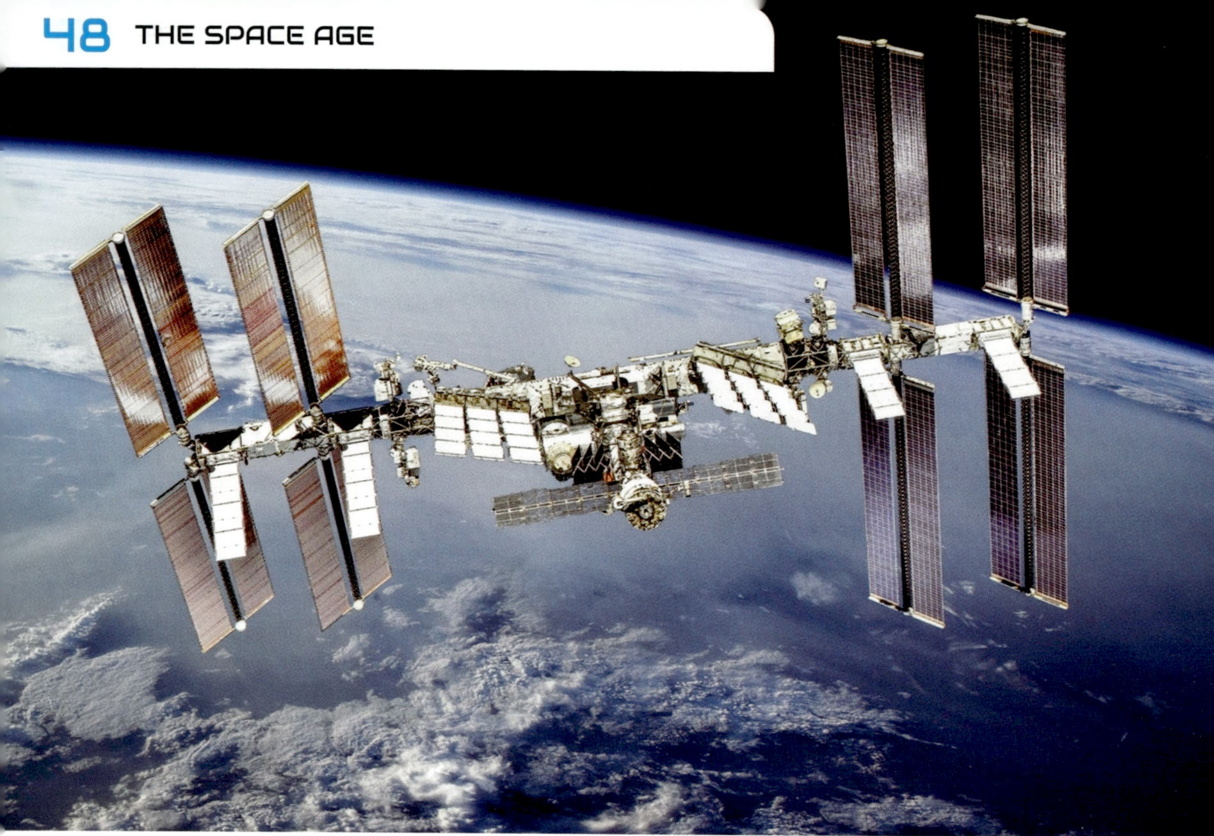

Electricity for space stations is provided by large solar panels, or arrays. These use the energy from the Sun to create an electric current. If laid flat, the International Space Station's solar arrays would cover half a football field.

Endeavour, were the backbone of the U.S. Space Program. They could carry out tricky satellite launches, repair and recovery missions, and even ferried a laboratory, Spacelab, into orbit. The shuttle made flying into space routine, but tragically *Challenger* exploded on launch in January 1986, killing the crew. Safety features were added, but in February 2003 *Columbia* was also destroyed as it reentered the atmosphere. The shuttle program was ended in 2011.

Space Stations

In the 1970s, NASA and its rival Soviet space agency turned their attentions to building satellites that were big enough for crews to live in for long periods, even permanently. The space station was born. Space stations are used largely as laboratories, where experiments can be performed in weightlessness and the vacuum of space.

The USSR launched the first station, *Salyut 1*, in 1971. This was followed by six further Salyuts and finally, in 1986, the Mir space station. Meanwhile, NASA created the *Skylab* project, based on technology developed during the Apollo missions. Skylab was visited by three missions during 1973 before burning up in Earth's atmosphere in 1979.

In 1998, construction of the International Space Station (ISS) began, a joint venture between many of the world's main space agencies, including NASA, the Russian Space Agency, and the European Space Agency (ESA), with smaller contributions from many other countries. The ISS has been permanently crewed by at least two astronauts since October 2000. The station is due to keep working until the end of 2030.

Space station technology has advanced rapidly. China launched two space stations (Tiangong 1 and Tiangong 2/3), which performed well during their lifetime. They completed a more ambitious space station in 2022. Living in space has been extensively researched. The longest any one person has lived in space is the 438 days spent by Russian cosmonaut Valeri Polyakov (1942–2022) on the space station Mir.

Space Flight Today

Space flight has never been more exciting. In 2017, NASA announced Artemis, a bold new plan to build a permanent base on the Moon, which will make possible human exploration of Mars. Meanwhile, private companies, such as SpaceX and Blue Origin, are playing an important role in developing powerful launch rockets. The space race has extended to Asia, with China and India competing to launch ambitious missions to the Moon and Mars.

SPACE STATIONS

Space stations contain everything needed to keep a crew in space for long periods. For example, *Salyut 1* consisted of four modules. There was a propulsion unit at one end with small rockets for moving the station in its orbit. The two middle pods had beds, workshops, and exercise equipment—astronauts have to exercise regularly to prevent their muscles wasting away in the weightlessness of space. There was an airlock and docking port at the other end where the astronauts' spacecraft attached. Later space stations had two docking ports, allowing supply capsules or visiting craft to dock. Since two craft could dock at the same time, the station did not have to be left unoccupied.

Space laboratories have been used to produce crystals and other materials undistorted by gravity, and to study the effects of weightlessness. In the future it may be economical to manufacture some materials and medicines in space.

SOCIETY AND INVENTIONS

Space Tourism

In 2004, the first private spacecraft, *SpaceShipOne* was launched into space. In October that year, the rocket plane became the first craft to fly into space twice in just two weeks. A similar launch system was then developed for taking paying passengers into space. In 2018 a larger model, called *SpaceShipTwo*, with room for six passengers and two pilots, was carried to 50,000 ft (15,000 m) beneath a jet-powered mothership (*White Knight Two*) before being released and powering to an altitude of 62 miles (100 km) using its rocket. After a few minutes in space, *SpaceShipTwo* glides back to the ground.

EXPLORING OTHER WORLDS

The Space Age has allowed people to explore the Moon, other planets, and the farthest reaches of the Solar System.

A montage of the Saturn system, showing the planet and its main moons. The images put together to create this picture were taken by space probes and sent back to Earth.

For thousands of years the other planets in Earth's Solar System were mysterious, distant objects. For the past few centuries it has been known that they are actually other worlds, but until recently these worlds could only be studied by astronomers using telescopes on Earth. The study of the larger Universe has also been held back by the atmosphere, which distorts light.

The Space Age changed all this. Since the 1950s, dozens of astronomical satellites have been put into orbit, where they can study light from the Universe in the vacuum of space. Even more ambitiously, space probes have been sent to all the planets in Earth's Solar System and beyond, into interstellar space.

The first Soviet astronomical satellite, Sputnik 3, was launched in May 1958. This mission carried a radiation detector and had an elliptical (stretched) orbit that allowed it to measure both the Van Allen Belts and cosmic rays in more distant space. Sputnik 3 also pioneered a new communications system that stored data over the entire orbit then transmitted it , or "dumped" it, to ground

LANDING ON THE MOON

The early Moon probes were crude devices designed to return data before crashing into the lunar surface. Landing a probe safely on the Moon was more difficult. Navigation and control had to be improved so that the probe could be placed on a suitable landing site (a relatively flat, firm plain), and additional rockets were needed to reduce the craft's speed as it neared the surface (the Moon has no atmosphere, so parachutes could not be used to slow the descent). These features added to the weight of the probe, so a more powerful rocket was needed to launch it. The first probe to make a soft landing on the Moon was *Luna 9*, launched by the USSR in January 1966. The probe took photographs and measured radiation, returning data to Earth by radio. The first soft landing on the dark side of the Moon was by China's *Chang'e-4* mission in January 2019. This landed in the Von Kármán crater. Communication with the module was maintained by the Queqiao communications satellite. The landing module was accompanied by a smaller yutu rover vehicle.

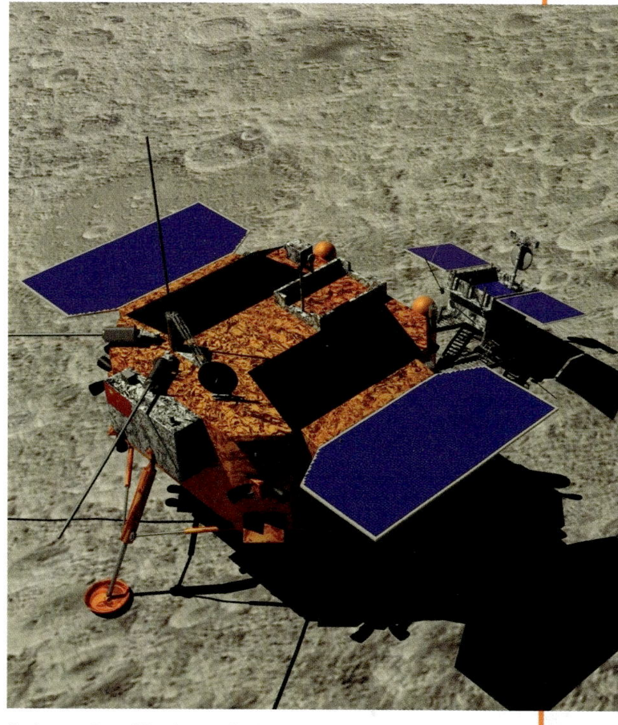

An impression of Chang'e-4 *on the far side of the Moon.*

Astronaut Charles Conrad (1930–1999) checks out Surveyor III, *a moon probe that had landed a couple of years before the Apollo spacecraft arrived in 1969.*

SATELLITE DISCOVERY

The very first successful American satellite, Explorer 1, carried an astronomical instrument—a radiation detector—built by James van Allen (1914–2006) of Iowa University. Van Allen hoped to study high-energy "cosmic rays," which almost never reach Earth's surface. But when Explorer 1 was launched in January 1958, the radiation detector went wild as the satellite orbited through certain regions. These were areas of trapped radiation and were named the "Van Allen Belts."

SOCIETY AND INVENTIONS

Life on Mars?

The idea that there might be life on Mars has fascinated people for hundreds of years. Ground-based telescopes were not powerful enough to shed much light on the debate, although some astronomers thought that they could see great networks of canals on the planet's surface, which they believed may have been built by aliens. The Viking probes, which visited Mars in 1976, found no evidence of canals or living things on the planet's surface. Since then, there have been about 20 successful missions to Mars. Scientists continue to look for evidence of ancient water and life. Between 2020 and 2024, scientists reported evidence of water in frozen lakes, rocks, and a deeply buried reservoir.

stations as the satellite passed over the USSR. From these small beginnings both NASA and the Soviet Space Agency launched many more satellites. Scientific satellites are one area of space in which scientists from many nations collaborate. Each satellite carries many separate instruments and experiments that have been devised at colleges and research institutes.

Probes to the Moon

The first spacecraft to reach the Moon was *Luna 2*, an uncrewed Soviet probe launched in 1959. A powerful rocket lifted the probe out of Earth orbit, and the precise timing of the launch meant that the probe swung onto a collision course with the Moon. *Luna 2* carried a range of scientific instruments and transmitted data back to Earth via a radio link. *Luna 3*, launched one month later, was even more successful, returning the first pictures of the far side of the Moon. Digital cameras had yet to be invented, and so the probe took a video with a film camera. The film was developed and processed on board before being scanned and transmitted to Earth by radio. Picture quality was poor, but Soviet scientists enhanced the images.

MARINER MISSIONS

The Mariner probes were the first spacecraft to be sent to visit another planet. *Mariner 2* (below) flew past Venus (the nearest planet to Earth) in December 1962. The probe's electrical power was provided by solar panels, and it was also equipped with a rocket engine for course corrections, sensors, cameras, and an array of scientific equipment. Scientists sent commands to the probe by radio. The probe used radio waves to look through Venus's thick clouds, revealing a extremely hot surface with temperatures of around 750°F (400°C).

NASA's next goal, a visit to Mars, was achieved by *Mariner 4* in July 1965. Throughout the rest of the 1960s and into the 1970s further Mariner probes visited Mars and Venus—*Mariner 9* actually went into orbit around Mars in 1971 and sent back detailed photographs of the planet's surface.

In 1974, *Mariner 10* became the first and only probe to visit Mercury. It flew via Venus, and used that planet's gravity to swing the probe onto a course past Mercury. This technique is called the gravity slingshot. *Mariner 10* also became a test vehicle for an even more revolutionary idea—the solar sail. By altering the tilt of Mariner's solar panels, scientists made the probe "sail" between orbits, propelled by the solar wind—a continuous stream of charged particles radiating from the upper atmosphere of the Sun.

VIKING ORBITERS AND LANDERS

The Viking probes of the 1970s gave scientists their first close-up look at the surface of Mars. The two probes were the most ambitious spacecraft constructed by NASA since Apollo. Each consisted of an orbiter based on Mariner spacecraft and a lander derived from the Surveyor Moon probes. The spacecraft weighed 7,758 lb (3,519 kg) at launch and were propelled out of Earth orbit by powerful Atlas-Centaur rockets. A computer on the orbiter then took over control of the spacecraft, using the positions of the Sun and the star Canopus to navigate. Information on the probe's position and status was relayed back to Earth by radio using the communications antenna. The probe was controlled by an on-board computer rather than an operator on Earth because radio signals (traveling at the speed of light) take almost 20 minutes to reach Mars from Earth. As the spacecraft approached Mars, the propulsion motor was fired, placing the vehicle in a stable orbit. The lander then separated from the orbiter and descended to the Martian surface, using parachutes and rockets to slow its fall. The orbiter completed a comprehensive study of the planet from space using two television cameras, a thermal mapper that could determine the surface and atmospheric temperatures, and a water-vapor detector that measured the amount of water in the Martian atmosphere.

The Viking lander carried cameras and equipment to measure weather and earthquakes. Its most important mission, however, was to search for signs of life. This involved collecting Martian soil with the sample collection boom and depositing it in the organic molecule detector. Moisture and nutrients were added to start any life processes, and changes in the sample chemistry were recorded. Some changes did occur, but scientists think that these were probably not due to living organisms.

The images sent back by the Viking landers showed that Mars was a cold, dry, and lifeless planet. The sky was shaded pink by the red dust that is blown into the atmosphere. The transmitting process for photographs worked remarkably well: the first transmission of an image began 25 seconds after landing. Most of the transmitting was done by a high-gain antenna that pointed toward Earth. Communication was either direct or via the orbiter.

Meanwhile, NASA was developing its own series of Moon probes—the Rangers, designed to crash into the lunar surface, sending pictures and other data back to Earth in preparation for the Apollo missions.

Missions to Venus and Mars

Earth is one of four small, rocky inner planets. The other three—Mercury, Venus, and Mars—are Earth's nearest neighbors in space and were the obvious next targets for space probes. NASA's Mariner spacecraft were among the first probes to fly past and orbit these planets in the 1960s and 1970s.

In the 1980s, NASA designed spacecraft to take an even closer look at our neighboring planets. Before this, most probes had been limited to high-speed "flybys," snatching a brief snapshot at the alien world and its moons. To obtain data over many months, a probe must go into orbit around the planet or even land on it.

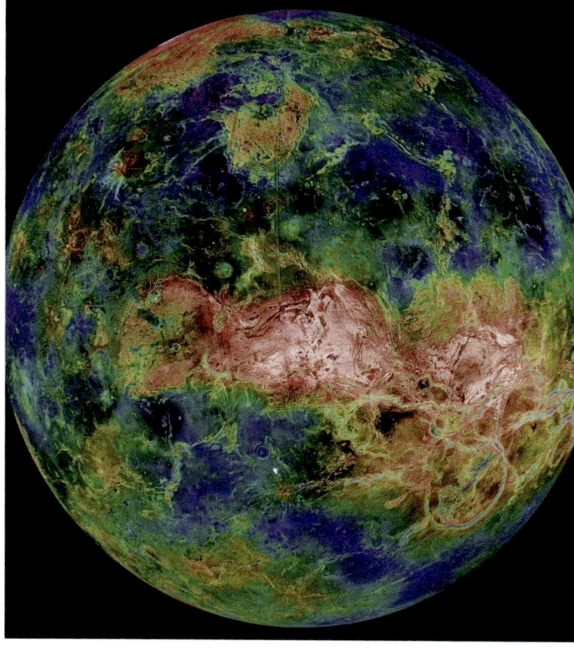

The surface of Venus, mapped by the Magellan *probe between 1990 and 1994. The probe then fell out of orbit, broke apart, and crashed into the planet's surface.*

OPPORTUNITY AND *CURIOSITY*

The *Opportunity* rover landed on Mars in 2004, a short time after the probe, *Spirit*, landed on the other side of the planet. The probes were powered by solar panels, which proved remarkably effective. *Spirit* operated for more than five years, while *Opportunity* continued to explore the red planet until 2018, which was 14 more years than expected. *Opportunity* was supplemented by the *Curiosity* rover that landed in 2012, and in 2025 it was still gathering data from the "red planet."

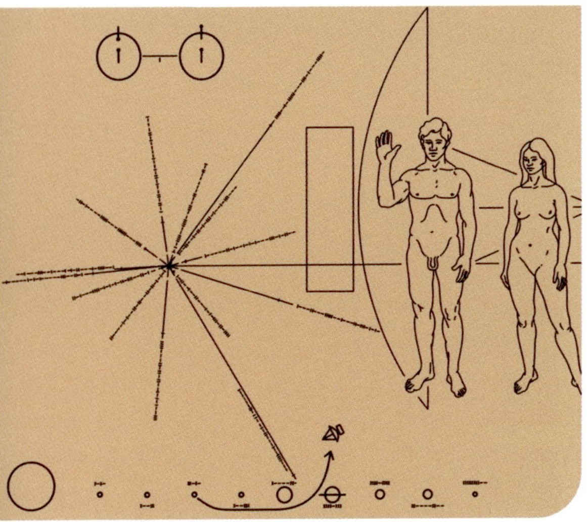

The Voyager and Pioneer probes carried a plaque showing who had made them and where they came from—just in case they were ever found by an alien civilization. The Voyagers also carried a gold audio disk that contained the sounds of animals, wind, the ocean, 90 minutes of music, and greetings in 55 Earth languages.

NASA's *Magellan* orbiter spent three years circling Venus, starting in 1990. To look through the thick clouds, it carried radar equipment used by remote-sensing satellites to map Earth. Scientists were able to turn this information into detailed maps of the planet's surface.

In 1997, the Mars Pathfinder mission delivered a small rover, called *Sojourner*, to Mars, the "red planet." The six-wheeled, solar-powered rover hit the surface inside a cocoon of large airbags, which inflated to break the fall once the lander had entered the atmosphere. In December 2003, a larger probe called *Spirit* landed on Mars using the same system. An identical rover, *Opportunity*, arrived a few weeks later in 2004.

The Mars rovers were sent commands by radio from the NASA control center, which took a lot of careful planning because of the long communication delay.

PIONEER AND VOYAGER

Pioneers 10 and *11* were modified versions of earlier Pioneer probes, which had been used to study the Sun. The low-cost project was designed to test conditions in the Solar System beyond Mars. The probes were controlled directly from Earth and spun in flight to give stability.

Voyagers 1 and *2* were much heavier and more complex than the Pioneers. Based on the Mariner probes, these craft were stabilized and controlled by an on-board computer because they were too far away to be remote controlled. Their instruments, including wide-angle and close-up television cameras, were mounted on a steerable boom that could be pointed in any direction. Because sunlight becomes very weak beyond Mars, solar panels could not be used, and both *Pioneer* and *Voyager* relied on nuclear generators for electrical power.

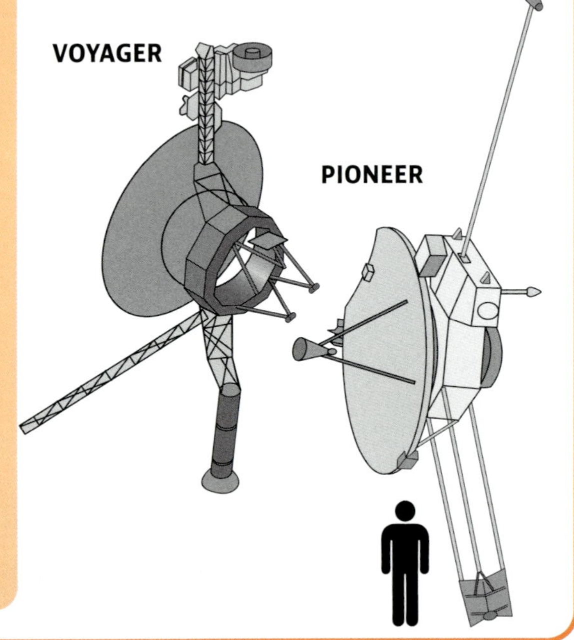

The rovers sent back detailed pictures of the surface of Mars and analyzed the chemicals in the Martian soil using on-board automatic laboratories.

From 2012, the *Curiosity* rover gave scientists a greatly enhanced picture of the structure of the surface of Mars. In 2020, China and the United States planned new rover missions to Mars.

Outer Planets and Beyond

The way to the outer planets was opened up by the Pioneer and Voyager probes launched by NASA in the 1970s. *Pioneer 10*, the first probe to visit Jupiter, arrived in 1973. *Voyager 1* reached Jupiter in 1979 and Saturn in 1980. *Voyager 2* took advantage of a rare alignment of all the gas giant planets—Jupiter, Saturn, Uranus, and Neptune—and visited each planet

FACTS AND FIGURES

This table gives the distances of the eight planets of the Solar System (and the dwarf planet Pluto) from the Sun.

Mercury	36 million miles	(58 million km)
Venus	67 million miles	(108 million km)
Earth	93 million miles	(150 million km)
Mars	142 million miles	(228 million km)
Jupiter	483 million miles	(778 million km)
Saturn	886 million miles	(1,427 million km)
Uranus	1,783 million miles	(2,870 million km)
Neptune	2,794 million miles	(4,497 million km)
Pluto	3,666 million miles	(5,900 million km)

THE SPACE LAUNCH SYSTEM

Bold missions need bold rockets. When NASA retired the Space Shuttle in 2011, it announced a much bigger replacement, the Space Launch System (SLS). The most powerful rocket ever produced by NASA, SLS is designed to carry a spacecraft, four astronauts, and up to 50 tons of cargo in a single mission. Although the first version is slightly smaller than the Saturn V rocket that sent astronauts to the Moon in 1969, it makes 15 percent more thrust (pushing force). It's also 40 percent faster, with a top speed of 24,500 mph (39,500 km/h)—over 100 times quicker than a Formula One car. SLS began its 25-day maiden voyage on November 16, 2022. The mission involved flying 280,000 miles (450,000 km) beyond Earth—more than 10 times the distance from New York City to Los Angeles.

The Space Launch System is the main launch rocket for the Artemis Moon landing program.

ION ENGINES

All rockets work on the same principle: they expel matter in one direction, and this pushes the rocket in the opposite direction. Chemical rockets expel hot exhaust gases but ion rockets expel a stream of ions (charged particles). Ion engines provide a lot less thrust than other rockets (they cannot launch a probe from Earth's surface) but are ideal for long journeys because they are very fuel efficient.

Ion rocket engines use electricity generated by solar panels to power their heating coils and other structures. The heating coils change the fuel into a flammable gas. The gas xenon, stored in the fuel tank in liquid form, is the fuel used by the probe *Deep Space 1*. A hot metallic grid then removes parts of the atoms (minute particles that make up all matter, including gases), turning them into positively charged particles called ions. The ions are focused into a stream, and then an electric field accelerates them from the rocket.

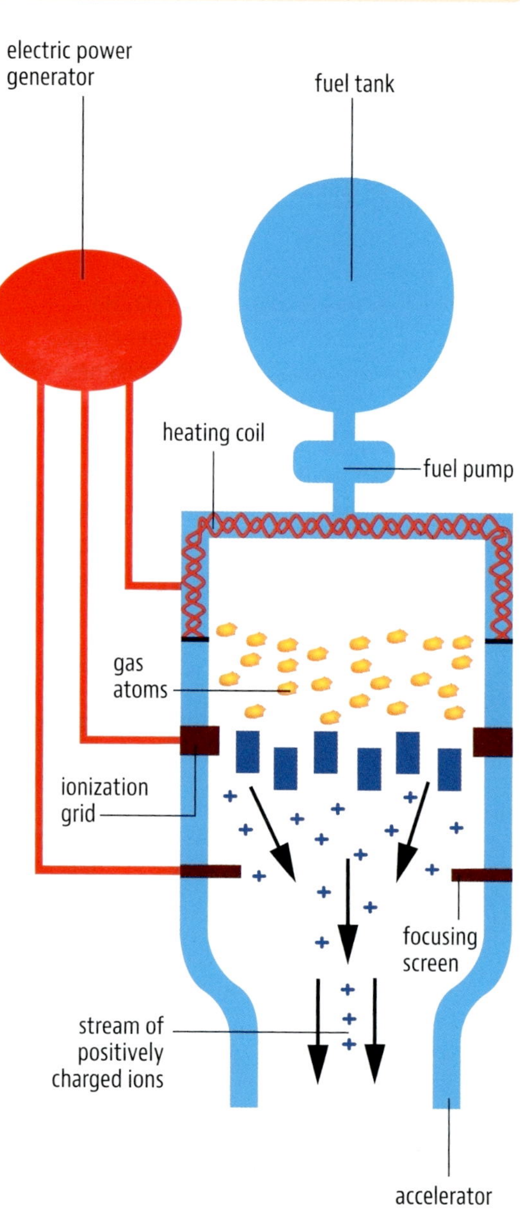

Deep Space 1, the probe powered by an ion engine, flew past the asteroid 9969 Braille in 1999, before changing course and visiting Borrelly's Comet in 2001.

in turn. It discovered various new moons of Uranus and Neptune, plus hitherto unknown ring systems. Both Voyagers have escaped the gravitational pull of the Sun and are now in interstellar space. *Voyager 1* is calculated to pass very close to a star that is 17.6 light years from Earth in about 40,000 years.

Other Missions

In 2001, *NEAR Shoemaker* became the first spacecraft to land on an asteroid, touching down on Eros, a giant rock that orbits close to Earth. In 2010, Japan's *Hayabusa* probe brought back dust from the asteroid Itokawa for analysis on Earth. In 2006, the *New Horizons* mission set off to study the outer edge of the Solar System. It sent back data on the dwarf planet Pluto in 2015, and in 2019 investigated another Kuiper Belt object, now designated Arrokoth.

Will humans ever be able to reach these outer planets? Currently, NASA has plans to send and land people on Mars by 2037, but this date perhaps seems overly optimistic and difficult to achieve.

The New Horizons *space probe has investigated the far reaches of the Solar System and sent back the first relatively close-range photographs of the dwarf planet Pluto.*

COMETS PROBE

When Halley's Comet flew past the Earth in 1986, there was a huge international mission to study it. Halley's Comet is the only bright comet that returns often (every 76 years or so), and so missions to it can be planned in advance. The European Space Agency's *Giotto* probe (right) carried a camera and several scientific instruments and flew within a few hundred miles of the comet's core. The spacecraft's base was covered by a thick shield made from Kevlar, an extremely strong plastic (used in bulletproof vests). This shield protected the probe as it entered the dust cloud produced by the comet's interaction with the Sun. *Giotto* also carried batteries that could provide electrical power to its experiments if its solar panel was damaged.

Giotto *sent back the first close-up pictures of the core, or nucleus, of Halley's Comet, showing the plumes of hot gas and plasma that erupt from the 7 mile (11 km) wide ball of ice.*

TIMELINE

1783 Marquis d'Arlandes and François Pilâtre de Rozier become the first aviators, flying 5.5 miles (9 km) over Paris in a hot-air balloon made by the Montgolfier brothers.

1783 A few months after the Montgolfier flight, fellow Frenchman, Jacques-Alexandre Charles flies to an altitude of nearly 1 mile (1.6 km), in the first hydrogen balloon.

1804 Sir George Cayley constructs the first working model of a fixed-wing aircraft.

1852 Frenchman Henri Giffard builds the first airship, or dirigible, powered by a steam engine.

1853 A full-size glider built by George Cayley carries a person on a short flight.

1896 Otto Lilienthal dies in a glider crash.

1903 Bicycle makers Wilbur and Orville Wright achieve the world's first controlled flight in a powered airplane.

1903 Schoolteacher Konstantin Tsiolkovsky suggests using rockets to reach space.

1907 The monoplane is invented by Louis Blériot; he later uses it to fly across the English Channel.

1910 Romanian engineer Henri Coanda builds a prototype aircraft that is powered by a jet of air. It never flies.

1912 American Glenn Curtiss builds the first flying boat, the *Flying Fish*.

1919 British airmen John Alcock and Arthur Brown fly across the Atlantic in a biplane.

1929 Robert Goddard launches the first liquid-fueled rocket.

1929 The *Graf Zeppelin* airship makes the first round the world flight, taking a little more than 21 days.

1930 Frank Whittle patents the jet engine.

1933 Boeing designs the first modern airliner, the 247.

1937 The *Hindenburg*, a hydrogen-filled airship explodes in New Jersey, killing many of its passengers. Airships are rarely used again.

1939 The first jet-powered airplane, the Heinkel He-178, is flown.

1939 The first practical helicopter is flown in the United States by engineer Igor Sikorsky.

1947 Chuck Yeager is the first person to fly through the sound barrier in the Bell X-1.

1954 The Convair XFY-1 Pogo Stick becomes the first V/STOL aircraft, followed later by the Harrier jump jet and V-22 Osprey.

1957 The first artificial satellite, *Sputnik I*, is launched by the Soviet Union.

1961 The USSR (now the Russian Federation) launches the first passenger-carrying spacecraft with astronaut Yuri Gagarin on board. American Alan Shepard is launched into space a few weeks later.

1962 Telstar, the first working communications satellite, is launched.

1962 The X-15 rocket plane flies at Mach 5, five times the speed of sound.

1969 NASA launches Apollo 11, the first successful crewed mission to the Moon.

1971 *Mariner 9* becomes the first spacecraft to go into orbit around another planet.

1976 The Lockheed SR-71 "Blackbird" becomes the fastest jet-powered aircraft, flying faster than Mach 3.

1983 The "stealth" fighter, or F-117 Nighthawk, is built by Lockheed.

1989 Voyager II passes Neptune, the outermost planet in the Solar System.

1998 Construction of the International Space Station (ISS) begins.

2001 The first tourist visits space. American Dennis Tito pays $20 million to spend 9 days aboard the ISS.

2010 The Japanese *Hayabusa* probe returns the first asteroid dust to Earth.

2015 *New Horizon* probe photographs PLuto.

2019 The Chinese lunar module *Chang'e-4* becomes the first uncrewed spacecraft to land on the far side of the Moon.

2021 The James Webb Telescope is launched; it will study how stars and galaxies formed and change over time.

2022 NASA's Space Launch System (SLS), an ambitious new Moon rocket, makes its first flight.

2024 China's lunar module *Chang'e-6* returns the first samples from the far side of the Moon.

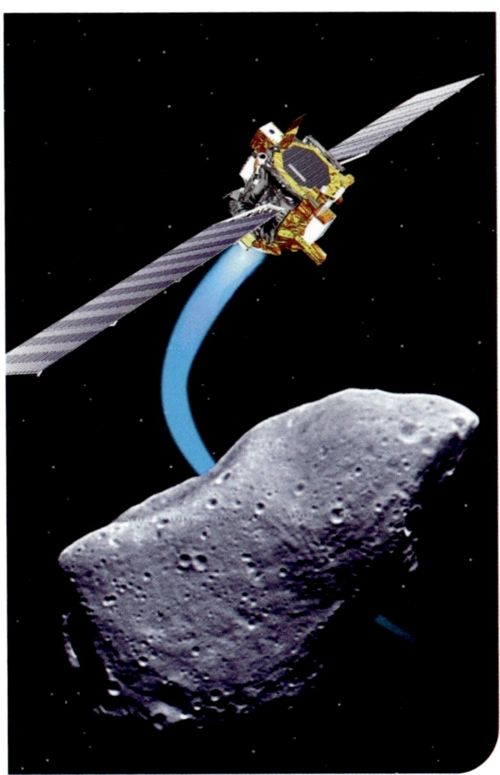

GLOSSARY

aerodynamic Able to move through a fluid (such as air) efficiently. Aerodynamic objects are shaped to reduce drag.

airfoil A shaped surface, typically curved on one side and straight on the other, that produces both lift and drag when moved through the air.

altitude The height of an aircraft or spacecraft measured above sea level.

ancient Greece A civilization that existed on the mainland and islands of modern-day Greece and Turkey between 2000 and 300 B.C.

asteroid A space rock that orbits the Sun. Most of the asteroids in the solar system orbit in the Asteroid Belt located between the orbits of Mars and Jupiter.

atom The smallest units in any substance.

aviator A person who flies an aircraft.

combustion When a substance burns. Engines burn fuel in combustion cylinders; rocket engines burn fuel in combustion chambers.

compression The act of being made more compact by the application of pressure.

dense A description of how much mass is packed into a substance. A handful of a dense substance, such as lead, weighs a lot. The same amount of hydrogen, which has a very low density, weighs much less.

drag A force that opposes the motion of an object through a fluid such as air or water.

drone An aircraft that has no passengers or crew, but is flown by a pilot on the ground.

fuselage The body of an airplane; it contains the cockpit and passenger cabin. Early aircraft had a basic frame for a fuselage. Modern planes use super-strong plastics and metals.

gravity A natural force that attracts two masses toward one another. Among its many effects, gravity draws objects toward Earth's surface and keeps the planets in orbit around the Sun.

hydrogen A highly flammable gas that is lighter than air. Pure hydrogen is uncommon on Earth. It is manufactured by breaking up water molecules into hydrogen and oxygen gas.

internal combustion The engine system used in cars and trucks, fueled by gasoline or diesel. Propeller planes use large internal-combustion engines.

interstellar Referring to the empty space between star systems. There are few large objects, such as planets or asteroids, in interstellar space. It is the emptiest place in the Universe.

Mach 1 The speed that sound travels through air in current conditions. The speed varies according to the temperature and pressure of the air, so Mach 1 is not a set figure. Mach 2 refers to double the speed of Mach 1. This numbering system is named for German scientist Ernst Mach (1838–1916).

microgravity The term used to describe weightlessness in space. Gravity is still acting on astronauts and the objects inside the spacecraft, but its effect in them is too small to notice.

orbit The path, shaped like a circle or an ellipse, that an object in space takes around another object.

ramjet A jet engine that does not have a turbine, but produces thrust as a stream of exhaust gases by burning fuel in a stream of air drawn in the front. Ramjets work best at very high speeds.

remote sensing A way of measuring or detecting things on Earth from the air or space using electromagnetic radiation or other waves. Remote-sensing devices are usually mounted on aircraft or satellites.

satellite A natural or artificial object in orbit around a star, planet, or other body.

solar panels Collections of solar cells used to convert sunlight into electrical energy. They are often used to provide electricity on spacecraft.

Solar System The Sun together with the eight planets (including Earth) and other bodies (such as dwarf planets, asteroids, and comets) that orbit it.

solid-fuel rocket A rocket in which the fuel and oxidant are both solids. Typically, solid-fuel rockets are simple metal tubes packed with a mixture of the propellants that are ignited to provide thrust. Solid-fuel rockets are less complex but more difficult to control than liquid-fuel rockets.

sonic boom The loud, thunder-like sound produced when an aircraft passes through the sound barrier.

sound barrier The abrupt increase in drag that occurs when an object approaches the speed of sound.

Soviet Of or from the USSR, a communist empire that existed from 1923 to 1990 and included present-day Russia, Ukraine, and Kazakhstan.

supersonic Traveling or capable of traveling faster than the speed of sound.

telecommunications Sending messages over a distance, usually involving electrical signals or electromagnetic waves.

thrust The force created by an engine that pushes an aircraft or spacecraft forward.

turbine A machine made up of a set of blades mounted on a central shaft. A moving fluid, such as steam or air, makes the assembly rotate. Turbines are often used to drive generators.

vacuum A space that contains no matter.

wingspan The distance from one wing tip to the other.

FURTHER RESEARCH

Books

Flight: The Complete History of Aviation by Reg Grant. New York: Dorling Kindersley, 2024.

Jobs in the U.S. Space Force by Kathleen A. Klatte New York: Rosen Publishing, 2025.

Space Exploration: A Short Illustrated History by Mike Goldsmith. New York: Rosen Publishing, 2025.

Web Sites

How the Wright Brothers invented fixed wing flight
www.Wright-Brothers.org

NASA, Student website
www.nasa.gov/audience/forstudents/index.html

Smithsonian National Air and Space Museum
www.si.edu/spotlight/aircraft

INDEX